TABLE OF CONTENTS

FOREWORD

The fall of the Berlin Wall in November 1989 is perhaps the most poignant symbol of the downfall of communism and the striving for freedom and democracy in the countries of Central and Eastern Europe. For over 40 years, the spirit of democracy in these countries was forced underground, rising briefly in 1956 in Hungary, in 1968 in Czechoslovakia and in 1980–1981 in Poland before being crushed. But the revolutions of 1989 have demonstrated that the desire for freedom did not die. The communist monopoly on power has been broken in every country in the region, sometimes with laughter, as in Czechoslovakia, sometimes with violence, as in Romania. Even in the Soviet Union, the first socialist state, the communist party has relinquished its leading role in society. The people have spoken.

Now the challenge facing the newly opened societies of Central and Eastern Europe is to build up the institutions of democracy and civil society, to create governments that are, in the words of Abraham Lincoln, of the people, by the people and for the people. The essays in this volume explore this challenge, and provide solid advice to the leaders, specialists and decision-makers in these countries, as well as insight for those in the West who wish to facilitate the process of democratization in the East. Western countries, as well as multilateral institutions such as the Conference on Security and Cooperation in Europe and the Council of Europe, can take steps to encourage the development of democratic institutions and civil society in the countries of Central and Eastern Europe. These issues are also examined in these essays.

The papers collected in this volume were originally presented at the meeting "Democratization, Institution-Building and Multilateral Cooperation in Europe" sponsored by the Institute for East-West Security Studies and hosted by the Polish Institute for International Affairs (PISM) in Warsaw March 1–3, 1990. The Institute for East-West Security Studies wishes to extend special thanks to Maciej Perczynski, Director

i

of PISM, and Miroslaw Miernik, Assistant Director for Conferences at PISM, for graciously hosting this meeting. The Institute would also like to thank the Ford Foundation, The General Service Foundation, The Hauser Foundation, The Rockefeller Brother Fund and the Rockefeller Foundation for their generous financial support of the conference and the publication and distribution of this Occasional Paper. Finally, thanks are due to Peter B. Kaufman, IEWSS Director of Publications, Mary Albon, IEWSS Publications Editor and Charlotte Savidge, IEWSS Publications Associate, for thier hard work in producing this high-quality publication in such a short time.

The 1990s will witness great changes in Central and Eastern Europe—changes resulting from the events of 1989. The process of democratization in the countries of this region will undoubtedly proceed in fits and starts, not without setbacks. The learning process has already begun. It is our hope that the essays in this Occasional Paper will provide some insight into the long and complicated proces of building democratic institutions that lies before us.

John Edwin Mroz
President
Institute for East-West Security Studies
May 1990

1

Introduction
PETER VOLTEN

The year of the bicentennial of the French Revolution witnessed another genuine revolution in Europe. Freedom of action at *the state level* in Eastern Europe has significantly increased. But, in large measure as a result of Mikhail Gorbachev's rise to power in the Soviet Union, the most dramatic and sudden changes have occurred at *the level of society itself.* The courageous struggle of underground movements like Solidarity and Charter '77, as well as the bold steps taken by Gorbachev, have awakened the hearts and minds of the peoples of Europe. The peoples of Eastern Europe have seized their own destiny and are demanding policies that until recently were forbidden dreams.

The repercussions of these internal developments on the international system have been directly visible and far-reaching. For almost half a century the political structure in Europe had been characterized by a robust, if not rigid, security system. Its dominant features had been the imposed divide between East and West. Ideological antagonism and a confrontation-oriented understanding of military security were given primacy over legal, cultural and economic relations between governments and virtually suppressed human exchanges between societies. Now, after the revolutions of 1989, governments *and* societies (which had done so long ago) have declared their willingness to construct a new political order in Europe based on principles and values of cooperation and mutual understanding. The challenge now has become how to implement those—internal and external—political goals in a peaceful and structured way.

Perhaps the most significant issue that will affect European stability is the ability to develop, at the domestic level, democratic institutions in the USSR and Eastern Europe. The central theme regarding the democratic process itself is the institutionalization of collective and individual rights and responsibilities. Among the main elements of inquiry are the role of political groupings (parties and interest groups including minorities); the constitutional definition of individual, social and democratic rights; the provision of a form of *Trias Politica*; and the degree of legitimization of the written and unwritten rules of the polity.

At the international level, the institutionalization of rights and responsibilities is a protracted process, starting with consultation and the exchange of diplomatic notes, and eventually leading to the formal adherence to international laws. Longterm, successful adherence by the polity to the rule of law requires a "sociopolitical" process which neither a central, legitimate authority nor constitutional rule can of themselves enforce. It is insufficient for newly democratizing societies to appeal to general international agreements like the UN Charter. However, certain general supranational institutions do exist and function well, such as the Council of Europe and its European Commission and Court of Human Rights.

One of today's challenges is to educate and demonstrate to societies the validity and usefulness of international institutions. Multinational "sociopolitical" developments, however slow they may be, have shaped Western Europe. This experience must be shared with societies in Eastern Europe and the Soviet Union as they begin to move toward integration with Western Europe and its democratic institutions.

In order to examine how the democratization process in individual countries in East Central, South East and Eastern Europe and a robust, integrated political system in Europe overall can be promoted, the Institute for East-West Security Studies has launched a series of seminars on "Democratization, Institution-Building and Multilateral Cooperation in Europe." Recognizing the different historical traditions of the East Central, South East and East European countries—which, for reasons of simplicity, are referred to under the rubric of "Eastern Europe"—and the Soviet Union as well as the different stages of transformation in these countries, the program first seeks to clarify and prioritize the various domestic and international processes. In specific, the program is attempting to:

- define desirable goals for the democratization processes taking place in Europe today;
- assess the current state of sociopolitical development in each country as well as the potential for cooperative multilateral activity;
- identify the most important areas in which democratization needs strengthening; and
- describe the actions national governments and the international community can take to strengthen democratic processes and institutions in Eastern Europe.

Bringing together leading European, American and Soviet experts to discuss the various aspects of these topics, the program will have a regular series of meetings to facilitate an ongoing dialogue on issues now undergoing dramatic changes.

At a meeting in Warsaw in March 1990 the group's task was to examine the broader, more theoretical aspects of the democratization issue, or, in short, to examine the question: "Transition from what to what?" Specifically, the aim of the seminar was to clarify the concepts of democratization and institution-building in Europe and to explore the linkages between numerous issues—e.g., politics and economics; civil society and communist heritage; revolution and evolution; state and society; national interests and group interests; democratization and security; and international institutions and the diffusion of domestic power.

The studies in this volume address various aspects of these issues from different perspectives of comparative approaches. *Ralf Dahrendorf* discusses the consequences of the collapse of the center and the problems arising from the replacement of administrative centralism by representative government. He examines the implications of an inevitable "economic valley of tears" and of the general time lag between economic and political transformations, as well as possible lessons from comparable experiences of peaceful transition in West Germany and Spain. As a central thesis, he strongly argues that the single most strategic need of the new democracies is the creation of the conditions of civil society described as "the common denomination of functioning democracy and an effective market economy." *George Schöpflin* concentrates on the historical-cultural basis for establishing viable democracies in East Central and Eastern Europe, comparing them with the conditions and experiences of Western Europe. He describes the different patterns of interest articulation, discusses the postrevolutionary relationship between state and society in terms of the legacy of the Soviet-type systems and summarizes the reasons for the widely varying foundations of political culture and self-confidence. *Samuel P. Huntington* places regime changes in Eastern Europe in the context of the global trend away from authoritarianism. He compares East European processes with the common features of the third wave of democratization which began in the mid-1970s, and analyzes the internal factors relevant to the stability of the new regimes. He also focuses on the impact of these transformations on the international system, and gives particular attention to the future role of a reunited Germany. *Eva Nowotny* examines the organizational and institutional framework for creating a new system of security, stability and cooperation in Europe. She places special emphasis on the role of the most comprehensive instrument of all-European integration, the Conference on Security and Cooperation in Europe, in the areas of all three of its baskets and to the growing scope of possible future tasks assigned to the Council of Europe.

In the present stage of both internal and international transformations in Europe, publishing anything on these subjects is like shooting at a rapidly moving and changing target. Nevertheless, an interim statement is necessary in order to identify as early as possible potential threats, real challenges and promising solutions to the historical change taking place in the early 1990s. If this publication contributes to the initial discussions and preliminary results in this early period of a redesigned Europe, then it will have already accomplished its task.

2

Roads to Freedom: Democratization and Its Problems in East Central Europe

RALF DAHRENDORF

■ *The Collapse of the Center*

The road to serfdom has been mapped by many, but the road to freedom leads through largely uncharted territory. To be sure, the language of such statements is not uncontested. What Friedrich von Hayek called the "road to serfdom" would have been described as emancipation by the followers of Marx who would also denounce as capitalist exploitation and bourgeois rule the freedom of democratic government and market economies. But one of the results of the events of 1989 is the "reunification of language." Few today employ the rhetoric of Marxism. Most admit that socialism, or at least communism, has turned out to be a form of serfdom rather than freedom, at worst a personal dictatorship, Stalinism, at best the leaden hand of an increasingly corrupt *nomenklatura*, Brezhnevism. Thus it is understood that the road to freedom is the path from administrative centralism to more open patterns of government and society.

This is what "we, the people" sought in East Central Europe in 1989; it was often given the name democratization. The immediate effect of the revolution of 1989 was, in all countries that were swept by its winds, the collapse of the center. This meant two things. First, the Party lost its political monopoly. Second, the economic planning mechanism lost its nerve center. (It is important to recognize that neither process has as yet occurred in the Soviet Union, which remains, for this reason as well as for several others, largely outside the scope of this paper.) The vocabulary used here is important: existing

5

structures were lost, they collapsed. The process was in the first instance a process of dismantling and destruction.

The consequences were and are serious. In the political sphere, the changes left a curious combination of a crumbling local and to some extent also central *nomenklatura* with governments which desperately try, and often fail, to get a grip on events. The East German case is extreme, largely because it emerges that there never was an East German state which deserves the name. In Poland, the reverse is true; a strong national culture seems to sustain a government which has set out on a courageous course of reform. But everywhere post-revolutionary governments find it hard to retain control. They are thwarted by problems of legitimacy, by the absence of a new institutional infrastructure, and by the continued presence of many agencies of the old regime.

The weakness of the political center is one of the causes of the return of old regional, ethnic and religious rivalries. (This is true in the Soviet Union as well, despite the fact that the central machinery of party and government has not collapsed to the same extent.) Impatience with the process of reform, a sense of relief about the removal of physical threats by the internal security forces as well as the Soviet army, and the absence of authoritative signals from the central government combine to encourage groups to try and go their own way. Sadly, one has to conclude that the more homogeneous countries are, the more likely they are to succeed in the process of democratization. Countries with an ethnically or otherwise divided population will probably be preoccupied for some time to come with their territorial integrity, and with the maintenance of law and order.

The collapse of the center is equally serious for economic developments. In an article in *The Wall Street Journal* (December 7, 1989), the financier-philanthropist George Soros described a condition (in the Soviet Union) in which the planning machinery is still in place, but has lost its brains, as it were. The heavy hand of bureaucracy prevents initiative, and is at the same time incapable of doing its old job of central direction, however ineffectually, so that nothing moves anymore. The lesson is not a happy one. Removal of tyranny does not by itself release the energies of freedom. At any rate it does not guarantee a constructive process of economic—or, for that matter, political—reform. In the first instance, it creates uncertainty, contradictions between remnants of the old and hopes for the new, and once the euphoria fades, misery and dissatisfaction.

This is, as it were, the starting point of the journey along the road to freedom in countries which have shed the yoke of really existing socialism. It sets the scene for formulating the main problems, and for giving some indications of possible solutions.

■ *The Democratic Deception*

One of the words which have returned to their old glamor in 1989 is democracy. Democracy was not only the goddess of Tiananmen Square but the hope of the people of Gdansk and Leipzig and Timisoara. It still is their aspiration. While it is not always entirely clear what is meant by democracy, certain features are generally recognized to be a part of the concept. Self-appointed leaders must be removed, the monopoly of one party broken. Instead there has to be a plurality of political groupings; there must be elections, and parliaments. Even these things, obvious as they may seem to many, are more easily said than done. It is therefore understandable that reformers tend to concentrate on the conditions for the first free elections. 1990 will see a number of such, in East Germany, Hungary, Czechoslovakia and probably Romania. But what happens after the magic dates?

The first point to be made here is trivial yet important; it is Churchill's familiar adage that democracy is a pretty bad system, except that all others are worse. Democracy is messy. Elections create as many problems as they solve, and sometimes more. Benevolent reformers in particular are likely to find that they do not command as much support as they think they deserve. "We, the people" may well wish to sweep away not only all those who are tainted by the old regime, but also the advocates of a third or middle way. On the morning after, a dreadful hangover may envelop not just the electorate but also the fledgling new political class. Coalitions may have to be cobbled together which have the seeds of their breakup built into their very construction. Some may even wonder—newspapers report that Lech Walesa has already made such noises— whether it would be better to keep, for a while, a tighter rein than is possible once one has had free elections.

It would not, I think. The force of democracy is unstoppable. But there is one critical point to be made about it which has

7

practical consequences. Many spokesmen of countries which have embarked on the road to freedom seem to believe that democracy—that is, parties, elections and parliaments—will give them signals about the future course to follow. Even activists think that it is sufficient to listen, and to listen to all who want to say something. In a number of countries, a confusing number of parties, including some self-declared non-parties (usually calling themselves "forum"), compete for popular support. All this is understandable, and laudable if one seeks to replace administrative centralism by representative government. But there is an attitude about that overlooks the second half of this phrase, *government*. Democracy is not just about giving expression to a wide variety of views, and creating a forum where all of them have their say. Democracy is a system of government. It is intended to make sure that those who govern have the support of the people, at least when they start; but by the same token it is about enabling people to govern. Parliaments are political institutions rather than mere fora for free expression. They must respond to proposals for change made by governments, or initiate such changes themselves.

I have heard a leading Hungarian politician reply to a question about his party's economic policy with the statement: "That is not for us to say but for the people." Such an approach will destroy democracy almost as quickly as it is created. Parties must provide the lead and try to persuade voters of their platform. If they win a majority, they must pursue what they promised until the electorate removes them from office and replaces them by another party. If there are constellations of parties, coalitions, they too must be clear about their intentions. Contrary to the literal meaning of the word, a functioning democracy is not the "rule of the people"; indeed there is no such thing. It is government put in place by the people and, if necessary, removed by the people, but it is government with a sense of direction.

The institutional consequences of this general comment are considerable. It is not surprising that a number of the new democracies are now introducing electoral laws which promise as much representation as possible. After one-party rule, people want to allow expression for every view, however small the minority may be which it represents. Thus there is a tendency toward total proportional representation without a threshold that keeps groups with less than 5 percent support out. (The additional question of giving voters the chance to reorder party lists is also relevant.) For the first free elections, this may be inevitable; but such electoral laws should not be entrenched in any way, for soon after the first election it will be necessary to consider the question of effective government. This probably requires either a threshold, or some form of electoral system which introduces a bias in favor of larger parties.

The other institutional consequence of regarding democracy as a form of government rather than mere representation has to do with the power of governments. Again, it would be understandable if there was an initial tendency to check and balance governmental power in every possible way. Again, however, it will soon become evident that unless governments are able to take the lead, stagnation and disenchantment will follow. There are several ways of strengthening government without endangering democracy. The German or British and the French or American methods are both viable; in one case, the head of government has certain constitutional prerogatives (*Richtlinienkompetenz*, or the right to dissolve parliament), but emerges from parliament; in the other, the president is independently elected to an office which entails real powers. There may be other methods.

The important point in this connection is not just the need to recognize that democracy is a system of government. There are also the special requirements of countries that are passing through a difficult period of transition. They may feel that they have just shed hated leaders and now want a rather less personal rule; they may distrust all leaders. But while such comparisons are misleading in part, it is worth pointing out that Germany's postwar transition owes much to the twin leadership of Konrad Adenauer and Ludwig Erhard, or that Spain after Franco would hardly have had such spectacular success without the combination of King Juan Carlos and to begin with Adolfo Suarez, later Felipe Gonzales. Transitions are immensely precarious processes in which the vision and the nerve of leaders can make a lot of difference, and constitutional arrangements must not prevent such leaders from doing what needs to be done.

■ The Economic Valley of Tears

The first substantive task of governments on the road to freedom is often economic. It is also extremely difficult and indeed painful. As we look at economic reform, it is even harder to generalize than in other fields. Each country has its own history, institutional structure and current condition, its own resources and realistic opportunities. One crucial point needs to be made at the outset for this very reason. Timothy Garton Ash mentioned in one of his brilliant descriptions of East European developments (he really is the great chronicler of 1989!) that the main economic-policy debate is one between Hayekians and Friedmanites. This is amusing but not funny. For one thing, the difference is important: Hayek is about economic systems, Friedman about economic policies. Both may be wrong, but it is easier to change policies than systems if one discovers that mistakes have been made. For another thing, it is critical to recognize that transition does not and must not mean a journey from one system to another. It is even misleading to speak of a transition from socialism to capitalism. The whole point of the road to freedom is that it leads from a closed to an open society. An open society is not a system, but a mechanism for exploring alternatives. It does not predetermine economic structures and policies but allows trial and error, mistakes and their correction. The first warning is therefore: please do not look for an alternative system!

To be sure, this does not mean that anything goes. Any central planning system which claims total control is incompatible with the open society. It is also, as we know, and as those who suffered from it have experienced at an enormous cost, ineffective. Elements of the market, of individual initiative, of incentives, of private property, are an indispensable prerequisite of a working modern economy. For East European countries, this involves major changes. Minister Balcerowicz in Poland has tackled them with great courage and a clear sense of direction. Perhaps, the group around Minister Klaus in Czechoslovakia will follow suit. Hungary of course has embarked on this route some years ago, though a lot remains to be done. Once again, the East German case is special in that the option of economic and monetary union with West Germany is now almost declared policy.

In all these cases, however, including East Germany, one feature of the economic transition deserves attention: it will inevitably lead through a valley of tears. The transformation of ill-functioning planned economies into growing market economies is not an immediate positive-sum game. At the very least, it requires a period in which wages remain constant if they are not falling, whereas hitherto political prices rise as subsidies are reduced or removed altogether. Goods begin to get into the shops but people cannot afford them. The probability is high that this process will be accompanied by unemployment, and also by the discovery that the much-praised net of social security in socialist countries is in fact very flimsy. Thus, things will get worse, in some cases much worse, before they get better.

This is one of the points where Western cooperation is critical. Indeed, the postwar Marshall Plan did exactly what is needed today; it filled in the deepest thought of the valley of tears and made the transition more bearable. If one wonders how long it is likely to take to get out of this valley, or at least to reach the upward slope where people begin to sense an improvement, it is once again doubtful whether there is a general rule. Ludwig Erhard was under tremendous pressure in West Germany three and even four years after the currency reform, when many argued that the rich were getting richer and the poor poorer. Felipe Gonzales took Spain through a period of over 20-percent unemployment and considerable suffering on the part of those voters who had got him into office, the workers: but in the end he just managed to win the second election after four years because things began to get better. If the objective is pursued with determination, four years may well be the period which it takes to pass through the valley of tears—and it is easy to see the conflict between this time span and the electoral cycle.

The critical conclusion from the two observations on economic reform offered here is probably that each country has to identify certain strategic changes on which it concentrates in the first instance. Changing everything at once—the currency, the system of ownership, external commercial relations, etc.—is likely to be too disruptive to be effective. It may make a valley of tears too deep for a country ever to reach the upward slope. On the other hand, making only minor adjustments is not good enough. Drastic changes are needed in particular respects. In the case of East Germany, this probably means monetary union with West Germany. In the Soviet Union, the key might well have been agriculture, with a combination of a price shock and private property; though the moment of change has probably been missed. I do not feel competent to judge where the critical changes should be applied in the other countries of East Central Europe, but would insist that strategic reform rather than system change or mere piecemeal engineering is needed.

■ *Politics and Economics*

One of the discoveries of the revolution of 1989 is that all accepted assumptions about the relationship between politics and economics are wrong. Curiously, Marxists and capitalists were agreed in their belief in the primacy of economics. Marx of course elevated this belief into a theory. He claimed that political revolutions would happen only if and when productive forces were held back by existing relations of production; revolutionary classes would draw their strength from suppressed economic opportunities. "We, the people" certainly wanted economic improvements in 1989, but the momentum of change was largely political. An implicit, and sometimes explicit, assumption of defenders of capitalism is that once market forces are allowed their sway, democracy is bound to follow. This too has turned out to be wrong, or at least overoptimistic. Perhaps the students on Tiananmen Square drew some of their strength from the fact that there had been a certain amount of encouragement of economic initiative in China; but then the clampdown was sadly effective. The process of democratization in the newly industrializing countries of South East and East Asia is very slow and painful. At the very least there is a time lag between economic and political reform, and as long as it lasts, unforeseen factors can intervene.

This is true for East Central European developments as well. The initial changes were political. Some leaders— possibly including President Gorbachev—may have hoped that political liberalization would by itself release economic forces of entrepreneurship and initiative; but clearly this was not the case. (It certainly did not happen in the Soviet Union.) A separate set of policies was, and is, required to set the sleeping forces of centrally planned economies in motion. I have argued in a lecture on "transitions" (in Gothenburg on August 31, 1989) that in fact all countries which have undergone success-ful transformations needed two leaders, one political and one economic. "Economic reformers need the protection of politi-cal leadership, and political reformers will only keep their open flank protected if they have a champion of economic policy by their side." Thus, it was Adenauer *and* Erhard, Gonzales *and* Boyer who accounted for the success of their countries, and we must hope that Mazowiecki *and* Balcerowicz, perhaps Havel *and* Klaus can one day be added to this list.

The issue is not just that two different impulses are needed to set the two processes of reform in motion. The deeper issue is that their time scales are different. New political institutions can be put in place within months, but economic reform takes years. The difference in time scales is significant. New political institutions need to establish their legitimacy; they have to be accepted and gradually anchored in the firm ground of a lasting political culture. Yet their first test is very tough. It is the test of the valley of tears. People are asked to accept that democracy begins with government policies which make their daily lives harder. Now that they are able to voice their grievances, they are asked to hold back and wait until the new institutions deliver the goods.

Even mature democracies would find it difficult to cope with such a condition. Indeed, if one follows the Arrow-Downs line of democratic theory, frequent changes of government would be a necessary consequence of the demand for long-deferred gratification. Thus, we must hope that Arrow and Downs, and Schumpeter before them, were wrong, and that political democracy is more than a quasieconomic process of maximizing support. There can be leaders, and objectives, which compensate for the temporary misery of economic circumstances. Clearly, this is a tall order. The incompatible time scales of economic and political reform are indeed one of the reasons why democratic institutions are likely to be shaky on the road to freedom. Only the second, and perhaps the third election will tell whether the new order has taken root.

■ *Prospects for Civil Society*

From one point of view then, the road to freedom is a race against the clock. It may take one year or less to introduce certain democratic procedures; it takes four years or more to grow the first fruits of economic reform; and until ten years have passed, we will not know whether apparent changes have become real. The French Revolution turned violent after two years and ended in a military dictatorship after seven. Those who prefer comparisons with 1848 do not

13

have much more evidence for comfort; the reaction set in almost immediately, and it lasted for decades. Perhaps the American Revolution offers the most hope, and of all the historical documents which one would wish to recommend as travel reading on the road to freedom, the *Federalist Papers* may well be the most relevant.

One concern which Alexander Hamilton, James Madison and John Jay had when they wrote their papers was the rule of law. They could see their way to a sensible structure for the legislative and executive powers, but they were wondering how one could establish the third great power of the judiciary, without delivering it into the hands of the others. "The want of a judiciary power" was above all Alexander Hamilton's concern (Federalist No. 22). How can its independence be safeguarded? And how can it be given the power to make its rulings effective? There are two obvious dangers. One is that newly democratic countries begin their course with acts of revenge on those responsible for the tyranny of the past, and the other is that the judiciary remains prey to political bias and control. In Latin America, several elected governments have made both mistakes; indeed the inability of establishing the rule of law is the greatest single weakness of most transitions to democracy on that continent. There are signs that Romania, and even East Germany, are making similar mistakes. I can but allude to the subject here; but perhaps were have written too much about democratic procedures and economic reforms, and too little about the rule of law and its preconditions. East Central Europe may have had too many visits by politicians and businessmen, and too few by lawyers.

The second lesson from the *Federalist Papers* has to do with James Madison's preoccupation with the real guarantees of individual liberty (notably in Federalist No. 10). Democratic procedures are all very well (says Madison) but as such they cannot protect minorities and individuals against the tyranny of the majority. What then can? Either a general acceptance of certain values—which however is too rosy an expectation considering the strength of self-interest—or the presence of numerous intermediate groups and agencies the interplay of which prevents the ascendancy of anyone, even of political majorities. What is needed, in other words, in order to give effect to the intentions of democracy, is the pluralism of civil society.

The word has become fashionable in Latin America, and now in East Central Europe too. This is to be welcomed. In order to do more than just write constitutions, and to build institutions, what is needed above all is the creative chaos of civil society. Indeed, civil society is the common denominator of a functioning democracy and an effective market economy. It is only if and when a civil society has been created that political and economic reform can be said to have credence.

But the task is daunting. Ideally, civil societies grow rather than being built. Someone sets up Harvard College, someone else establishes the Republican Party, someone different again starts publishing the *New York Herald*, and so on. In the emerging democracies there is neither the time nor the wherewithal to wait until this happens. A degree of deliberateness is needed to build autonomous organizations and institutions which mediate between government and the individual. Foundations have a role to play in this process, and it is pleasing to see that some are emerging in East Central Europe with the help of their equivalents elsewhere. Small businesses are of course a part of civil society; it is therefore critical to provide the legal and financial space for their creation. Media are important features of civil society, and one must hope that the new monopolists of the Western media can be prevented from establishing their regime in the new democracies.

It is naturally pleasing for Western intellectuals to see their East Central European friends play such a prominent part in launching their countries on the road of freedom. What could be better than a professor of medieval history as the leading parliamentarian in Poland, a playwright as the President of Czechoslovakia, a conductor as the hope of many in East Germany? Yet it is not sour grapes which lead me to sound a note of caution. Independent intellectuals are also an indispensable element of civil society. In order to work, a free country needs critics who are not tied into the structures of power. During the process of transition, intellectuals may have to hold office; but only when they can return to their desks are we able to conclude that the institutions of civil society have been safely established.

One further concept needs to be introduced at this point, namely, citizenship. The rediscovery of citizenship in the revolution of 1989 links the new democracies with the old ones in the OECD world. Without the basic equality of citizenship, modern democracies cannot work. Moreover, this means not just equality before the law. Civil rights and political rights of citizenship have to be backed up by certain social rights. There has to be a common floor of chances of participation, and a clear limit to the ability of those in exalted positions to control the life chances of others. Citizenship means the abolition of privilege as well as the creation and maintenance of universal entitlements.

Civil society is not perfect anywhere, nor is it ever secure. Its creative chaos will forever annoy governments that will therefore try to impose a false sense of order on it or to destroy it. The rule of law is frequently under threat. Ironically, in view of the fears of the authors of the *Federalist Papers*, it is not the importance of the law but its abuse for private gain which threatens the rule of law in the United States. Citizenship rights have suffered in a decade which has placed all the emphasis on economic growth and neglected those who did not benefit from its gains. In any case, civil society will forever remain an unfinished task, as is right and proper under the conditions of openness which mark the road to freedom. But a start has to be made; and if there is a central thesis to this paper, it is that the single most strategic need for the new democracies is to back up both political and economic reform by the creation of the conditions of civil societies.

■ *The European Challenge*

It would be wrong to conclude this brief analysis of some of the problems of democratization in East Central Europe without at least a reference to the international conditions in which the process takes place. In the beginning there is the "Sinatra Doctrine": the Soviet Union has said (through President Gorbachev's spokesman Gerasimov) that the former communist satellite countries of Eastern Europe must be allowed to "do it their way." The Brezhnev Doctrine is dead. As one listens to people in Eastern Europe, one hears nothing so often as the statement that "we have not left the East in order to join the West, but in order to join Europe." Thus the challenge of creating conditions that allow the process of democratization to continue is to no small extent one for Europe.

In one respect, that diverse and somewhat amorphous entity, Europe, has already taken up the challenge. One may surmise that the way in which the European Community has got its act together in the 1980s has contributed to the plausibility, if not the possibility, of the revolution of 1989. Even Europe 1992, the project of the Single Market, was and is important, because it embodies the prospect of an alternative to the military and political blocs of yesterday.

It is particularly pleasing that the president of the European Commission and his colleagues, as well as most heads of government in the Community, have recognized that under the changed circumstances of 1989, the project of the single market by 1992 can be no more than a beginning. A door has to be opened wide first to the remaining EFTA countries and then to the countries of East Central Europe. It is too early to tell how exactly the invitation to come through that door and join the party will and even should be couched, but the fact that there will be such an invitation is clear.

This is only the beginning. Two subjects are likely to dominate the European agenda in the years to come; one is money, and the other, security. I have assumed that monetary union between the two German states will come about at an early date. The process of monetary integration in the European Community is moving forward. Convertability is likely to be high on the agenda of every single East Central European country. One can foresee a European monetary space of considerable economic and political significance. Some envisage similar developments in the field of security. At a recent symposium which I chaired (organized by *Die Zeit* in Hamburg on December 2, 1989), Henry Kissinger put forward ideas which seemed to amount to the notion of a "Central European Treaty Organization," no less. This is probably some way away. But the factual dissolution of the Warsaw Pact, and the evident need to reconsider the objectives of NATO, may generate ideas which contribute further to the construction of a common European home.

This will be a home without superpowers. It will not extend to the Soviet Union, let alone from San Francisco to Vladivostok. Yet it will have to define its place in a new international structure. There are moments when one feels that we have once again reached a point at which there is a chance to reconstruct a world order. But as soon as one begins to embrace that idea, one also remembers the seriousness of the threats to this opportunity. The Soviet Union may well be too preoccupied with its internal problems to have much time for the world. The United States has already developed a curious mixture of presence and remoteness so far as the events of 1989 are concerned. And within Europe, much still needs to be accomplished, not least the completion of the map of, and above all the march along, the road to freedom.

3

The Prospects for Democracy in Central and Eastern Europe
GEORGE SCHÖPFLIN

Prolegomena. This essay is concerned with the problematic of establishing viable democracies in the post-communist states of Central and Eastern Europe. It starts from the assumption that there is nothing in the political culture, social structure or totalizing experience of these polities that makes the creation of democracies inherently impossible, but argues that there are serious political obstacles to this course, not to mention economic ones. Having said this, however, there is a likelihood that over the coming few years, the nascent democracies of the region will differ in a number of identifiable ways from those of Western Europe and that it will take some time before these basic obstacles are dissolved. And given the policy implications of these propositions, it is further assumed in this essay that maximum clarity about the nature of the obstacles to democracy in Central and Eastern Europe is beneficial to all parties. A final assumption is that the changes that took place in Central and Eastern Europe in 1989–1990 were predicated on the conviction that democracy as practiced in the West was the most effective political system and, indeed, that there was no alternative to it.

■ Democracy and the Definition of Interests

Western democracies have as one of their central characteristics the primacy of material interests and this is crucial in structuring the political game in such a way as to ensure a high degree of stability. By focusing on material interests, liberal democracies are able to weather quite serious

19

challenges to the ruling government, but within a broad acceptance of the political framework, which is flexible enough to
accommodate both material and nonmaterial contests. The argument about the primacy of material interests is, essentially, that
emphasis of this kind provides clarity and predictability, which
allow for a relatively smooth debate over the allocation of
values and resources.

Material interests can be straightforwardly defined and
reciprocally understood; appropriate institutional and legal
provisions can be made for their equitable validation; and they
offer a relatively easily comprehended means of determining
individual and group aspirations. It is, of course, to be understood in this connection that groups and individuals have
numerous crosscutting and overlapping interests, so that the
identification of interests is never absolute. Individuals must
reckon with the competing aspirations of production and consumption, short term and long term, individual and collective
goods, etc., when calculating their interests and acting politi-
cally as a result.

While material interests have primacy, they do not exclude
nonmaterial values; they merely displace them to a subordinate
position. Nonmaterial values and the identities that derive
from them are as various as material ones. They can include
competing claims for allegiance from nation or religion or
gender or race or status or a host of less easily categorized
possibilities, such as morality or the environment or compassion or loyalty to community and the like. These can and
frequently do color the definition of material interests, often
distorting them out of calculable shape, but they do not eliminate them entirely.

■ Material and Nonmaterial Interests

The debate in a polity may in fact be struc-
tured around the assertion or denial of the primacy of material
interests and/or the insistence that nonmaterial values must
have priority, but this almost invariably remains at the rhetori-
cal level and is, in reality, perceived and negotiable in material
terms. Hence when a section of the community calls for greater
public spending for the "disadvantaged," this demand may be
legitimated in terms of compassion, but the reality is that this is
a sectional interest making a claim for greater allocation.

On the other hand, the role and function of nonmaterial

interests in liberal democracies is not to be underestimated. They provide expression for the affective dimension of politics, for the storehouse of values that cement the bonds of loyalty which ensure that a community remains a community and not just a disparate collection of individuals; for the external boundaries that separate one community from another; for the structure of past and future that is essential to sustain a community; and ultimately for the elements that constitute the moral universe by which individuals and groups establish what is to be regarded as positive and negative, right and wrong, good and evil.

However, while the existence of nonmaterial interests is essential to maintaining a community in being, they can become dangerous to political stability if they achieve primacy in the political game. Whereas material interests are easily subjected to bargaining and negotiation, where concessions can be made and recouped elsewhere in an identifiable fashion, this does not hold for nonmaterial interests. On the contrary, precisely because nonmaterial interests have roots in the affective dimension, they cannot be readily conceded, as they tend to be regarded as the central, constitutive core of a community's identity. It takes a major upheaval to shift the thresholds of a perception to such an extent that a community can actually give in on an affective interest, e.g., defeat in war, revolution, a fundamental change in power relations, etc. When this does happen, one is witnessing the signs of a political system in crisis and, as a matter of routine, such concessions would not be made over the bargaining table, or else only exceptionally. Arguably, the Soviet Union passed this threshold early in 1990.

It should be evident from the foregoing that too salient a role by nonmaterial values results in solid alignments by those concerned and these cannot become the subject of negotiation. Hence the necessary fluidity, the give-and-take that is the hallmark of liberal democracy, is blocked. Northern Ireland is an illustration of what happens when material interests are subordinated to nonmaterial ones—the problem becomes intractable and not capable of resolution by bargaining.

■ The Legacy of Soviet-Type Systems

In Soviet-type systems, however, this clarity of interest articulation is absent. Indeed, one of the central reasons for the transformation was that the intertwining of the political and the economic spheres was fundamentally distorting the articulation of interests and thereby making it impossible to make the most rational use of resources. But matters went beyond this. One of the most important features of Soviet-type systems is that the political sphere encompasses all others, to such an extent that all actions and transactions are actually or potentially politicized. The master of the political sphere, the communist party, is not, of course, a "party" in the Western sense at all, in that it is not a representative of a partial interest. Rather, it seeks to be the sole organ of interests aggregation, which it is supposed to achieve through its monopoly possession of perfection.

This thoroughgoing assimilation of material interests under communism has had the inevitable result of making it extremely difficult for individuals and groups to define their interests and identities. The corollary is a variety of ways of self-definition by nonmaterial criteria, in which material factors are subordinated to the demands of nationhood or religion or morality or whatever. The difficulty with this is, as implied in the foregoing, that nonmaterial interests are far more difficult to bargain with, that the political debate inevitably tends to become heavily charged with emotional appeals, that the definition of what is and is not relevant to a particular political issue is enormously extended. By the same token, appeals for popular support are now made primarily on nonmaterial grounds and this almost automatically brings a degree of arousal with it. That, in turn, makes quiescence a much harder task and is likely to impact on a range of other issues.

A case in point is that of Serbia under Slobodan Milosevic, who transformed the political scene with his fiery, nationalistic rhetoric, which basically sought to offer a remedy to the severe economic problems of Serbia by placing the blame for these on the perceived pressures on Serbian nationhood from non-Serbs. This had the desired effect of generating enormous support for the Milosevic line. It enabled him to silence his critics and to reassert Serbian power over the Albanian-inhabited Kosovo and the multinational Vojvodina. On the other hand, it did nothing to solve Serbia's economic problems. And by extending the issue from the socioeconomic question of Serbian hardships to one of Serbian nationhood, Milosevic and his supporters placed the future of Yugoslavia on the agenda as the non-Serbs increasingly resented his strategy of reasserting Serbian power.

The proposition in this essay is that until the primacy of material interests is established in the post-communist states of Central and Eastern Europe, the chances are strong that their politics will be governed by constant appeals to nonmaterial interests, which will reverberate in the affective dimension, and produce patterns of arousal and quiescence that will be relatively unstable. Thus parliamentary coalitions could well prove to be short-lived, as their members opt out on issues of "conscience" or "morality" or "honor"; and it will take time for politicians and parties to define themselves by material interests.

Ironically, the time that this process will require is likely to be determined by the purposiveness of particular governments in introducing a thoroughgoing dissociation of the market from politics. This, however, will require of these governments that they act in a way that gives material interests primacy, which is precisely the difficulty. In practical terms, the transformation of a hyper-étatist system into a market system will generate massive tensions and these will be tailor-made for political intervention by appeals to nonmaterial interests. The prospect is for many years of more or less instability.

■ *New Political Parties*

The way in which political parties are emerging from the Soviet-type miasma and the kinds of parties that are being established seems to bear out this somewhat pessimistic prognosis. Essentially two patterns are visible—conglomerates and fragments. Conglomerate parties are coalitions clustered around some nonmaterial interest, while fragments are mini-parties, presumably with no great political future. The ordering principle of such a coalition is that its members unite around some nonmaterial principle.

Thus Solidarity has emerged as the representative of Polish society in opposition to the communist party (that no longer exists). Its *raison d'etre* is to provide a powerful counterweight to the ruling Soviet-type party and this continues even when that Soviet-type party has shed its particular characteristics. Thus the symbolic message of Solidarity is that there is a real Poland that it and it alone represents. This, of course, is predicated on a highly homogeneous concept of Polish society, in which there are no major cleavages and overlapping or crosscutting interests, which is manifestly not the case. In the short term, the existence of a conglomerate is probably beneficial, as the society in question must have time to rearticulate itself.

An analogous process can be observed in the GDR, where a party using Social Democratic colors increasingly emerged as the dominant force in the early months of 1990. In Hungary, both the Democratic Forum and the Alliance of Free Democrats could claim to be conglomerates, while in Bulgaria the transformed communist party appeared to be dominating the stage, using both left- and right-wing elements.

Fragments are more straightforward. As the political scene opened up, the number of tiny parties mushroomed. These claimed the allegiance of small groups and were often barely more than single-interest pressure groups. The chances were strong that they would be swept away as larger parties were consolidated, presumably through absorption.

A final problem area in this connection was the likelihood that, in reaction to the overmighty states with which these politics had been saddled under the communists, the new orders would place excessive emphasis on parliaments. Thus rather than opting for classic separation of powers and checks and balances, the governments would be largely subordinated to legislatures and would find it difficult to govern. In Hungary, where this danger was acute, the situation was further exacerbated by the introduction of a referendum, which could be triggered off by a relatively small number of signatures. The introduction of the rule of law, independent judiciary and even a constitutional court would not be sufficient to offset this excessive concentration of power in the legislature.

■ *State and Society*

The key problem of 20th-century democracy is what roles are to be assigned to the state and to society. The traditional European principle was that society is creative and the state is reactive. However, this no longer has complete validity; indeed, it may not even be a rebuttable presumption. Consequently, much of the political debate in democracies is, at a deeper level, concerned with continuously defining and redefining the relative role and powers of state and society. The state has assumed a variety of roles in the name of society—as arbitrator, regulator, goal-setter, executor and interest aggregator. All of this is founded on the assumption that the state is neutral, that it is a kind of platonic agency capable of determining the "public good" by criteria obscure to anyone else or that it is simply carrying out the wishes of society as expressed through the legislature. Indeed, the socialist agenda is in large part based on the belief that the state can substitute for society and is the best, most capable agency for introducing and administering equality.

The problem with this supposition is that it does not reckon with the autonomy of the state. The state is not, in reality, a neutral actor, but has interests of its own that it seeks to validate and implement, at times in the teeth of opposition from one or other social group. These can then be legitimated in the language of social provision or clarity of administration or whatever, so that for all practical purposes the state pursues political objectives its own.

In two particular areas this is palpable. States will do everything they can to safeguard their budgetary allocations and to prevent transparency about their operations by denying information to the public. When the state is overlarge, it will tend to generate a dynamic that is antagonistic to autonomous economic activity, as this will threaten the power of the state and thus curtail the operation of the market. Furthermore, the state is by definition non-productive, so that its activity must be financed by society. In effect, this means that the state is parasitical on society, both through its routine extraction of resources and in that if the state becomes the dominant activity in a particularly polity, if it becomes the "glittering prize," then talent that might go into economic enterprise is siphoned off into state service.

Other tensions in the relationship between state and society are wide-ranging and complex. There is, for example, the problem of perceived fairness. If state provision is opaque and unequal, but has acquired a kind of legitimacy through time, then an attempt to amend it may result in social tension. This becomes particularly acute at a time of major social or political or economic or technological change, which will inevitably produce new winners and new losers. The countries of Central and Eastern Europe are self-evidently in this situation and will be for some years.

The contradictions between state and society are far-reaching and ultimately beyond resolution. This implies that there has to be a balance between the two and the location of the balance changes over time. It is in this connection that an open democratic system proves its superiority to closed ones. The boundary between state and society is more readily negotiated in an open system than in an authoritarian one.

This does not mean, of course, that all conflicts can be resolved by a democratic system. Indeed, the strength of democracy is more that it provides opportunities for the renewed raising of old questions, in new forms, that it accepts that no solution is final, however it may be packaged at any one time. In this sense, democracy is a continuing debate about the limits of politics, about the criteria for the allocation of values and resources, about the relationship between state and society, about individual and collective provision and about the particular levels and forms of inequality that can and do arise.

The difficulty for the countries of Central and Eastern Europe is that their particular experiences of the last four decades do not predispose them to view these problems with equanimity, all the less so given their mounting economic plight. A perfectly plausible scenario is to suggest that growing sections of the new losers will associate their losing status with democracy and the market and will be vulnerable to authoritarianism. The constriction of interests enforced by the Soviet-type system will prevent them from gaining any broad view of their interests and identities in the new system. This, coupled with the propensity for affective mobilization discussed previously, and the political inexperience of societies that have been depoliticized, can result in impatience, unfulfillable expectations and possibly governments that will be at a loss when confronted by pressures of this nature.

One of the peculiar legacies of Soviet-type systems is that Central and Eastern European societies are simultaneously demanding extensive state protection and individual freedom. Given that the old system was directed at protecting individuals from the economic consequences of their economic actions, the auguries for stability are not good. The mixture of high levels of dependence on the state and diminishing resources will require very sophisticated skills of crisis management for the strategy of marketization and thus individual responsibility to succeed.

Hence the attraction throughout Central and Eastern Europe of the Swedish model. This is not derived from a real

Sweden, but from a mythicized version of Sweden, where there is supposed to be prosperity, social peace, high levels of state protection and international neutrality. For all practical purposes, the attraction of Sweden should be equated with a myth of social harmony.

It will be seen from the foregoing that in this present analysis the key function of democracy is regarded as relatively equal access to resources and the way in which this is defined. Those responsible for providing these definitions, indeed for constructing the agendas, are, of course, the intellectuals. This particular social formation has long played a role, from before the onset of communist rule, of being a surrogate public opinion, parliament and opposition. In this context, therefore, their role in the coming period will be vital, given that they will define the aspirations of society. Hence the particular emphasis to be given to what individuals can expect under the new system acquires enormous significance, at any rate in the short term.

■ *The Role of Intellectuals*

Intellectuals in Central and Eastern Europe have long played a political role going well beyond their ostensible function of determining the agendas of the future and subjecting the present to systematic analysis. For all practical purposes, they have been a surrogate opposition, a substitute parliament, a channel of public opinion and, as they have defined it themselves, the conscience of the nation.

In the aftermath of World War II, the legitimation of communism was in large part the work of the intellectuals. Throughout Central and Eastern Europe, the most visible and most self-confident group of intellectuals were those of the left. Those of the center and the right, including Christians, were silenced by the trauma of the war and the association of their ideas with Nazism. In this respect, left-wing intellectuals had the field very much to themselves and their role in the construction of the intellectual aspects of Soviet-type communism cannot be underestimated. This is not, of course, intended to imply that they were solely responsible for imposing communism on Central and Eastern Europe, that was not the case. Nevertheless, for a generation the intellectual hegemony enjoyed by the left, and that came to include the various attempts to reform official Marxism-Leninism as well, was unquestioned.

By 1989, however, the relationship between intellectuals and the left in Central and Eastern Europe was severed. With hardly a dissenting voice, the intellectuals of this region had opted for democracy and were extremely influential in bringing it into being. The support they gave, the way in which they interpreted events and structured their arguments, the criteria they established the alternatives that they put forward and so on were suffused by a commitment to democracy; in turn, this made a nondemocratic alternative virtually unthinkable.

All this raised a question, however. Was the intellectual stratum strong enough to sustain democracy? It is generally agreed that democracy requires the committed backing of a middle class if it is to have a chance of success and this middle class is customarily defined as a bourgeoisie, an entrepreneurial class, with an economic interest in democracy. However, the particular problem of the countries of Central and Eastern Europe in this connection is that the Soviet-type system eliminated the bourgeoisie, which in any case was small before the takeover. It cannot be reconstituted overnight.

That, in turn, raises further questions. Can the intellectuals sustain democracy on their own? The answer is probably not, for they are not strong enough economically and their constituency, the world of ideas, does not make them best suited for this role. Nor do they seem well placed to call into being the entrepreneurial class that democracy needs. The tension between intellectual and entrepreneurial modes of thought and action has been fully documented—it is one of the most fundamental cleavages in modern European history. The intellectual pressure for clarity of thought and, possibly, moral purity in action is again not the best basis for constructing democracy, which is all about compromise.

There is a further and even deeper problem here. Let us assume that the currently triumphant intellectuals of Central and Eastern Europe are sincere and genuine in their commitment to democracy and are determined to make it work even to the extent of promoting the rise of an entrepreneurial class and living with the lack of moral and intellectual clarity that democracy requires. But beyond that there remains the problem of the intellectuals themselves. If democracy in Central and Eastern Europe acquires the qualities and characteristics found in the West, the chances are excellent that the present role and status of intellectuals will decline if not fade entirely.

As democracy takes root, the traditional role of intellectuals as the conscience of the nation is bound to decline, simply because the nation will have genuinely representative institutions through which to make its desires known. There is almost an element of pathos in the question of whether, to bring democracy about, the intellectuals are prepared to sign their own death warrants as a high status reference group.

In essence, one of the central questions posed by the great turning point in European history that was 1989 was whether the intellectuals of Central and Eastern Europe would be prepared to abandon their long-established primacy in politics and turn politics over to the people. In other words, will they act as democrats or is their commitment to democracy restricted to words? For the time being, the evidence (see below) is that they are likely to be reluctant to do so, but this may well change over time, particularly when economic issues create opportunities for genuine representation from below.

■ *Language and Politics*

The control exercised by intellectuals is effected primarily by their control of the language of public discourse, something that they continuously contested with the ruling communist parties. The impact of communism on the cultures of Central and Eastern Europe and especially on their political languages requires special study and what follows here can be no more than an initial attempt to sketch the outlines of the problem.

The core of the problem is that a totalizing system generated its own totalizing language through which it sought to suppress expressions of autonomous thought and behavior and to substitute its own alien patterns on it. This applied above all to the language and crucially the expression of alternative visions of the future. The underlying dynamic of Soviet-type systems was relatively straightforward. They erected their own particular variants of all of those and declared them to be the sole possible modes of expression; disagreement was excluded neither by ideology, which simply declared the superiority of Marxism-Leninism, or by coercion.

The political monopoly of Marxism-Leninism was paralleled, therefore, by a monopoly of the communist meta-language. The monopoly grew thinner and thinner as Marxism-Leninism lost its content in the 1970s, after the invasion of

Czechoslovakia, and assumed the role of a facade for the exclusion of alternatives, an instrument of censorship. But this had its impact on intellectual discourses, because those who wanted to make an appearance on the public stage were perforce obliged to make some obeisance to it. Inevitably, there was some rapprochement between the two languages and this is still perceptible in the way in which ideas are expressed in Central and Eastern Europe.

The kind of patterns that have survived include the emptying of certain words of their content—"socialism" being the most obvious—and the emergence of certain linguistic forms, notably the convoluted sentence structures, the employment of vague abstractions, pleonasm and above all the preference for complexity over simplicity. The need to evade censorship has brought with it an inclination toward an allusive, tangential style, often extremely complicated, in which what is not stated is more important than what is. It is as if in the struggle to cleanse the language of Marxist-Leninist vocabulary, those involved had to an extent succumbed to the disease, albeit in a milder form. The coming of democracy has not resolved this problem overnight, especially as this complex mode of expression has its precommunist antecedents.

The problem raised here also relates to the difference between high cultural languages and demotic modes. The intellectuals who have controlled the high cultural modes have traditionally made major efforts to keep this for themselves and to prevent the emergence of simple public languages. The irony of the previous state of affairs was that by being engaged in continuous conflict with the communists, the intellectuals were at the same time also involved in a tacit arrangement with them to exclude the bulk of the population from political participation. Insofar as political debate existed, it took place overwhelmingly in the languages monopolized by the party and the intellectuals.

The situation is now, of course, under notice of change, but there is no guarantee that the intellectuals will adapt immediately to the demise of communist power and the communist language. It will clearly take time for a new, more accessible, more demotic language of public discourse to be fashioned and many intellectuals will resist the process. Yet without such a development, which the intellectuals will define as vulgarization, democracy is hard to envisage.

■ Historical Experiences

Western Europe in the 1990s can look back on four decades of prosperity, effectively functioning democracies and political stability. The perception of these is fused in the eyes of Western opinion and consequently the general prestige of democracy is very high. It was not always so. In the interwar period, significant currents of opinion looked askance at democratic systems and were tempted by the seeming dynamism of left- and right-wing totalitarianism. The profound difference between then and now is that totalitarian solutions have demonstrably been proved to be an utter failure—those of the right in 1945 and those of the left in 1989.

To add to this picture it should also be noted that superpower tutelage in Western Europe was relatively benign. The United States did not seek to impose its system and culture on Western Europe in the same crass way that the Soviet Union ruled Central and Eastern Europe. Naturally enough, U.S. influence and pressure were strong and resented at times, but crucially in this context they operated in such a way as to permit West Europeans a good deal of leeway to develop their own patterns. This has been vital to the recovery of Europe in the 1990s and to the winding up of the baneful legacy of the Great European Civil War of 1914–1945.

The broad pattern of the West European experience has been structured around an economic system widely described as "capitalism," but in reality a mixed economy in which the state has played a role of increasing significance, despite the post-1980 attempts to cut back on state power. This, coupled with a competitive political system, has offered most groups sufficient access to power and opportunity for the satisfaction of aspirations to create not only relative stability, but also a fair degree of resilience to absorb pressures from disgruntled social groups or new political actors. Thus these systems were able to weather dismantling of outdated industries (coal, steel) and the emergence of ethnically based political movements.

The weakness of this system, on the other hand, is that by concentrating on material values, it has largely overlooked the need for some agreement on broadly shared nonmaterial values. Consumption is not in itself sufficient and the apparent emptiness, the 'goallessness' of Western culture has been widely condemned. At the same time, it is also true that the absence of a single such collective value is almost certainly a factor of stability, in that it precludes the excessive emphasis on one value and the potentially emotional responses that could be generated on this basis.

Finally, the Western states have constructed fairly strong systems of legitimation based on the past. The element of historic continuity in underpinning these systems is important, though not exclusive. Indeed, the European tradition simultaneously stresses continuity and revolution as constitutive elements in its systems of values, and it moves from one to the other according to circumstances. Importantly, the discontinuities of the Western tradition have been relegated to the more remote past and are not a part of the active present. The way in which the bicentenary of the French Revolution was celebrated in 1989 is a case in point.

The countries of Central and Eastern Europe have a very different tradition to look to. They lack the self-confidence that comes from four decades of having operated a successful system; on the contrary, they have had to live with the historical memory of having had an unsuccessful, alien system foisted on them. The very unmixed Soviet-type system, which treated private economic activity, i.e., the market, as a criminal or semicriminal activity, and merged the economic, legal, social, etc., spheres into the political, left the individual unprotected. Consequently, there remains considerable suspicion of the state, of politics and political activity and a certain propensity to accept instant solutions on the part of sections of the population.

The experience of failure is another negative factor. Although the system that failed was widely seen as alien and offensive to national traditions, nevertheless no one likes to be associated with a bankrupt enterprise. And even if most people regarded the Soviet-type system as illegitimate, they still had to live with it and make their personal compromises with it. At one level, this inevitably associated them with the failure too, regardless of whether they were party members or not. This tends to promote a defeatist attitude and a certain irresponsibility, in that if no one is to be made accountable for the failure, the entire concept of accountability will be weakened.

Whereas Western Europe enjoyed a fairly continuous tradition of democracy—or at any rate feels that it does—this is viewed as a luxury in Central and Eastern Europe. The Great European Civil War, which brought destruction and dislocation to Western Europe, was an unmitigated catastrophe to the East. So, by way of example, the frontiers of the West European states were not altered very significantly between 1914 and 1945. To the East, there were unbelievable frontier shifts and demographic changes. No Western city suffered as much damage in World War II as Warsaw. This dislocation impacted with particular force on the prospects of creating viable democracies, in that it is difficult in the extreme to build a democratic system in the absence of civil society and civil society is hard to bring together where the basic solidarities that come from long-established, stable social coexistence are missing.

To these should be added the very different experience of superpower tutelage. The Soviet Union did not, in Churchill's celebrated phrase, "let the small birds sing," but insisted that all the countries under its control imitate it down to the last rivet. This brought a humiliation and another source of discontinuity, especially as the national traditions were in any case less robust than those of the West. The experience of Soviet power, with all its ramifications, will continue to reverberate through the political cultures of the countries of Central and Eastern Europe for some time to come. It is hard to see the kind of synthesis between European and American values that has come about in the West taking place further east. If anything, their experience will prompt the countries of the East toward a slavish imitation of things Western, regardless of the cultural context from which they sprang. The superficial signs of this may be viewed in Budapest, where Pierre Cardin, Adidas and McDonald's have already established themselves on the elegant Váci utca.

Finally, on the negative side, though without placing too much emphasis on this, there is the much quoted factor that the polities of Central and Eastern Europe have never been able to organize working democracies, and that the systems existing between the wars varied from the highly pluralistic Czechoslovak republic to the medieval Albanian kingdom. The significance of the absence of democracy before communism cannot be dismissed entirely, but it is the contention of this essay that the events of the last 40 years were far more influential. Having said this, the memory of the precommunist period is likely to play a role, in that it will be taken as an exemplar, a period when everything was supposed to be "good," unlike what followed. In other words, the past is likely to become a legitimating myth and is potentially valuable in this role.

The most cogent factor in pushing one toward a favorable prognosis for the introduction of democracy in Central and Eastern Europe, however, lies in the determination of the newly arrived political elites to install it, and in their conviction that there is no alternative. In essence, they derive their legitimacy both from the collapse of the Soviet-type systems and from the fact of having made a revolution, whether of the "gentle" kind in Czechoslovakia or the rather more violent one in Romania. The positive aspect of this is that the situation can prompt new governments to sweep away the past and to opt for far-reaching innovation. Poland is pioneering this path.

This room for maneuver can be used to insist to sometimes skeptical populations that there really is no alternative to democracy and that flirting with the authoritarian temptation is likely to lead into the cul-de-sac of history. Ultimately, though, the support of the West for the experiments in constructing democracies out of the ruins of left-authoritarian regimes—a much harder task than the equivalent out of right-wing authoritarianism—is vital for their success. The West will have to show considerable patience with the initial difficulties that the countries of Central and Eastern Europe are likely to undergo in their painful journey to democracy.

4

Democratization and Security in Eastern Europe
SAMUEL P. HUNTINGTON

■ Introduction

Fundamental political change is occurring at two levels in Eastern Europe. At the national level, the communist regimes have collapsed and their societies are attempting to create new, more democratic political systems. At the international level, the security system that was imposed after World War II is disintegrating and new patterns of international relations are emerging. These two developments—the breakdown of national communist regimes and the breakup of the international communist order—stem from many causes. The decline of Soviet power is the primary cause of the second and an important contributing cause to the first. The regime changes in Eastern Europe are also, however, part of a worldwide movement away from authoritarianism and toward democracy. The East European changes produce a double vacuum. The Leninist regimes are disappearing but they have not been replaced. The hegemonic power has retreated and apparently abdicated, but no new source of international order has emerged. The central issue is: How will these two processes of disintegration at the national and international levels interact so as to affect future political stability and international security in Europe?

This essay does not answer this question. It does, however, attempt:

1. to place regime changes in Eastern Europe in the context of

the global trend away from authoritarianism[1] and to identify possible future political developments in Eastern Europe;

2. to summarize the changes in the East European international system and to identify ways in which it may evolve; and

3. to set forth some of the implications of these two processes for stability and security.

■ Global Democratization and Eastern Europe

Democratization in the modern world has occurred in waves. The first or long wave began in the United States in the 1820s and ended after World War I, encompassing many northern and central European countries, the British settler colonies and some Latin American countries. Austria, Poland and the Baltic states established democratic institutions in the last phase of this wave. Beginning with the march on Rome, a 20-year reverse wave led to the replacement of many democratic regimes with authoritarian ones, including all those that had been established in Eastern and Central Europe. The Allied victory in World War II and Western decolonization produced a second, short wave of democratization which ended about 1960. This wave penetrated Eastern Europe only as far as the American and British armies did in 1945. A second reverse wave got under way in the early 1960s and lasted until the early/mid-1970s, affecting much of Latin America as well as other countries (e.g., Greece, the Philippines, Korea, Nigeria). Reflecting the flood and ebb of these waves, the number of democratic countries in the world was roughly: 26 in 1922, 11 in 1942, 39 in 1962, and 29 in 1973.

---

1. Throughout this paper, the term "authoritarian" is used to refer to all regimes that are not democratic. Democratic regimes are those whose most powerful collective decision-makers are selected through open, competitive, fair elections in which the bulk of the population is eligible to vote. Authoritarian or nondemocratic regimes in the contemporary world are usually military regimes, personal dictatorships, one-party states or some mixture of the three. Most communist regimes have been one-party systems, although Romania under Ceausescu and North Korea under Kim Il Sung were primarily personal dictatorships. Poland in the 1980s was an interesting mixture of a decaying one-party system ruled by a military officer who exercised considerable personal power and was also secretary general of the Communist Party. Communist regimes may be more or less totalitarian. In the 1980s Romania closely approximated the totalitarian model while Poland was considerably distant from it.

A third wave of democratization began in 1974 with the end of the Portuguese and Greek dictatorships. The following year the death of Franco began Spanish democratization. In the late 1970s, the democratic wave spread to Latin America. During the next decade democratization occurred in Ecuador, Peru, Brazil, Bolivia, Argentina, Uruguay, Guatemala, El Salvador, Honduras, Panama, Chile and, in some measure, Mexico. In the mid-1980s the wave rolled on to the Philippines, Korea and Taiwan in East Asia but was brutally stopped in Burma and China. Meanwhile, India entered into and then gave up emergency rule; Turkey replaced democratic government with military rule and then returned to democracy; while Nigeria did the opposite and returned to democratic government but then suspended that and returned to military rule. Pakistan voted the opposition party, led by a woman, into power. South Africa liberalized its social and political system, then halted the process and suppressed black opposition, then once again renewed the process. All in all, apart from Eastern Europe, two dozen countries shifted from strictly authoritarian regimes to primarily democratic ones during the 15 years after 1974, and in 1989 about 50 countries had some form of democratic institutions. Eastern Europe was thus the fourth major geographical-cultural region—after southern Europe, Latin America and East Asia—to be swept by the democratization wave. As in the first wave, democratization came to Eastern Europe after it occurred in many other countries and as a part of the breakup of empire.

The causes of third-wave democratizations varied from phase to phase, from country to country, and from time to time. Five factors, however, were widely prevalent in causing movement in these transitions to democracy: legitimacy decay; economic development and reversal; Catholicism; external actors; and demonstration effects. These factors were present in Eastern Europe as well as elsewhere.

After World War II democratic norms became widely prevalent in the global community, and hence authoritarian regimes faced great difficulties in legitimizing themselves. Military regimes typically attempted to do so by promising eventual return to democracy and by promoting economic growth in order to achieve "performance legitimacy." Revolutionary regimes and communist regimes appealed to ideology. Over time these sources of legitimacy weakened. The legitimacy of many regimes was undermined by economic reversal and that of the

Portuguese, Argentine, Greek, Philippine and Soviet regimes by military reversals. The legitimacy of the East European communist regimes, of course, suffered from the start as a result of their imposition by the Soviets. During the 1950s and early 1960s fairly rapid rates of economic growth bolstered these regimes, but by the 1970s growth had stagnated. Their legitimacy was undermined by the inefficiencies and corruption of their centrally planned economies just as the economic reversal resulting from OPEC oil price hikes and unwise economic policies undermined the legitimacy of authoritarian regimes elsewhere. Warsaw Pact regimes, apart from Romania, were also unable to appeal to nationalism for legitimacy.

Second, a very strong correlation exists between level of economic development and democracy. Hence transitions to democracy are likely to occcur among countries in the middle or upper-middle levels of economic development. About two-thirds of the third-wave democratizations of non-communist systems happened in countries at those levels. In almost all countries, with Poland perhaps being the major exception, the movement toward democracy was in large part led by the urban middle class produced by economic development. In the late 1960s Franco's planning minister, Lopez Rodo, said that Spain would become a democracy when its per capita GNP reached $2,000. It did, right on schedule (with an assist from Franco's death). In 1976 Spain and Greece had per capita GNPs over $2,000. So also, according to World Bank figures, did Czechoslovakia, the GDR, the Soviet Union, Hungary, Poland and Bulgaria. In 1976 the East European communist countries were, on the average, wealthier than the non-communist countries that transited to democracy in the third wave beginning in

Table 1
Economic Wealth and Democratization

GNP per capita 1976	Countries Democratic in 1974	Non-communist Democratizers 1974–1989	European Communist Countries
Over $3,000	18	0	2
$1,000-$3,000	4	11	6
Less than $1,000	3	10	1

Source: Economic data—World Bank, *World Development Report, 1978*, pp. 76–77; political classifications—Samuel P. Huntington.

1974.[2] The basis for democracy in terms of economic wealth, in short, existed in Eastern Europe.

Third, before 1970 a high correlation existed between Protestantism and democracy. The third wave, however, was in large part a Catholic wave, beginning in Iberia, sweeping through Latin America, and moving on to the Philippines. The reasons for this Catholic predominance go back to Pope John XXIII, Vatican II, and the fundamental changes in the Church at the grassroots in many countries, all of which produced increased opposition by bishops and priests to authoritarian rulers. In countries such as the Philippines and Chile cardinals played active political roles in bringing about regime change. In Eastern Europe, the two most Catholic countries, Poland and Hungary, were the lead countries in democratization. Although Cardinal Glemp followed an accommodationist policy, the Polish Church provided the institutional bastion for opposition to the regime and religious legitimacy to that opposition. In addition, and most important, of course, the election of a Polish pope introduced a major new force in the political equation. Throughout the third wave, Paul VI and John Paul II seemed to have a knack for showing up in full pontifical majesty at crucial moments in the democratization process in countries. If, as Timothy Garton Ash has argued, one had to choose a single date for the "beginning of the end" in Eastern Europe, it would be the Pope's "first great pilgrimage to Poland" in June 1979. "Here, for the first time, we saw that large-scale, sustained, yet supremely peaceful and self-disciplined manifestation of social unity, the gentle crowd against the Party-state, which was both the hallmark and the essential domestic cata-

---

2. Economic comparisons between market and centrally planned economies should be treated with a large grain of salt. After 1976, indeed, the World Bank gave up the effort to provide data on nonmembers with planned economies. These data problems should not, however, invalidate the general point about the relation between the economic development levels of European communist countries and third-wave democratizers. In a corroborating analysis several years earlier, Phillips Cutright established a strong correlation between level of communications development and democracy, and used this to highlight anomalous cases far off his regression line. The principal European countries that were much less democratic than they "should" have been, according to his analysis, were Spain, Portugal, Poland and Czechoslovakia. See: World Bank, *World Development Report, 1978* (Washington, 1978), pp. 76–77; Phillips Cutright, "National Political Development: Measurement and Analysis," *American Sociological Review* 28 (April 1963), pp. 253–264.

lyst of change in 1989, in every country except Romania (and even in Romania, the crowds did not start the violence)."[3]

A fourth set of causes of the third wave were the changes in policy and actions of major external actors. The European Community provided support for and incentives for democratization in Spain, Portugal and Greece. Congress began to change U.S. policy toward human rights and democratization in the early 1970s. This change was vigorously carried forward and expanded by the Carter and Reagan administrations and had a major impact on democratization in Latin America and the Philippines. Similarly, Gorbachev's reversal of the Brezhnev doctrine and his support for leadership changes in Eastern Europe were clearly critical to the regime changes there. The Polish transition of 1988–1989 apparently derived primarily from internal developments. In August 1989, however, Gorbachev reportedly intervened to urge communist party leaders to join in a Solidarity-led government. Later that fall, the Soviets did not object to the Hungarians opening their border with the West and Gorbachev's visit to East Berlin triggered the removal of Honecker. The Kremlin made clear that Soviet troops would not be used to put down the protests in Leipzig and other cities. With respect to Czechoslovakia, Gorbachev reportedly urged change on Jakes and Adamec in the summer of 1989. In November the Soviets indicated they would repudiate the 1968 invasion, thereby delegitimizing the Czechoslovak party leadership, and strenuously warned Prague against using force to prevent change. The Soviet policy change led to highly nationalistic pro-democracy demonstrators chanting "Gorby! Gorby!" in the streets of Leipzig, Budapest and Prague, and to Mikhail Gorbachev joining John Paul II, Jimmy Carter and Ronald Reagan as a major transnational promoter of democratic change in the late 20th century.

A final cause of some democratizations is the impact of earlier democratizations. The Spanish and Argentine transitions encouraged other regime changes in Latin America; the Philippine transition stimulated that in Korea; the Polish and Hungarian changes helped set in motion events in other East European countries. When the East Germans moved in October, simple national pride required the Czechoslovaks to move

---

3. Timothy Garton Ash, "Eastern Europe: The Year of Truth," *The New York Review of Books*, February 15, 1990, p. 17.

in November. Earlier changes become an independent, external cause which can lead to efforts to reproduce democratic transitions in countries where the social and political conditions may be hostile. The Philippines and Korea had that impact in Burma and China. The earlier East European transitions triggered the demonstrations, repressive response and violence in Romania and have stimulated demands in the Soviet Union for similar political changes. Demonstration effects may make the democratic spirit willing, but they do not create the social, economic and political muscle to make democracy a reality.

East European processes of transition share many common characteristics with other third-wave regime changes. All successful transitions, however they were initiated, involved negotiation and compromise. A common theme was the willingness on the part of the major participants to let bygones be bygones and to pursue policies of moderation and reconciliation. From the "Revolution of the Carnations" in Lisbon in 1975 to the "Velvet Revolution" in Prague in 1989, they also were characterized by minimal violence. The politics of the transitions typically involved four sets of players: those for and against democratization in the government and those for and against democratization in the opposition. In cases of regime *transformation*, the initiative came from reformers in the government; Spain, Brazil, Chile, Taiwan and Hungary tend to fit this model. In cases of regime *replacement*, the authoritarian regime collapses or is overthrown and the democratic opposition comes to power; Portugal, Argentina, the Philippines, East Germany and Romania tend to fit this model. In still other cases of *transplacement* that fall somewhere in between, democratization is the joint product of government and opposition groups; Uruguay, Korea, Poland and Czechoslovakia approximate this model.[4]

---

4. Statements by East European opposition leaders suggest that large numbers of them wish to go to Sweden by way of Spain. The Hungarian transition is, however, the only East European transition that significantly resembles the Spanish transition. The Polish transition does not because Jaruzelski was at best a reluctant democrat. He was not a Polish version of Juan Carlos or Suarez, whereas Pozsgay certainly aspired to be and in considerable measure has been. For the Polish-Spanish comparison, see Anna Husarska, "A Talk with Adam Michnik," *The New Leader*, April 3–17, 1989, p. 10.

The ending of the authoritarian regime is, of course, only the first phase in the political transition. A democratic regime has to be installed and then consolidated. Consolidation is still under way in most third-wave countries. Initial steps have involved the creation of new constitutional structures providing for an elected parliament, an elected executive or one responsible to parliament, and an independent judicial system. Equally important is the development of political parties and a political party system which combines, in some measure, responsibility to the public and the capacity to govern. A democratic system may be said to have been fully institutionalized when it passes a two-turnover test: that is, when one duly elected party or coalition turns over power to a duly elected successor party or coalition and this second elected government then also voluntarily gives up power after losing an election. Several new democracies have passed a one-turnover test; very few, Portugal being the most notable example, have passed the two-turnover test. East European countries are obviously in the very preliminary stages of this process.

In Eastern Europe the collapse of communism is a fact; the creation of democracy remains an aspiration. Assuming democratic institutions do come into being in Eastern Europe, what are the prospects for their consolidation and for political stability? The record of consolidation of third-wave democracies in Latin America and elsewhere suggests that the following factors are likely to be relevant to the stability of the new East European regimes:

1. The extent of the country's previous experience with democracy. In Eastern Europe, Czechoslovakia is in the lead with Romania and Bulgaria at the other extreme.
2. The level of social and economic development of the country. Czechoslovakia and East Germany have the advantage here.
3. The success of the authoritarian regime. Peoples who make a success of authoritarianism appear to be more likely to make a success of democracy. No East European country rates high here, but East Germany and Hungary are probably in the lead.
4. The extent, depth and strength of independent social and political organizations. Poland is uniquely advantaged with respect to this factor.
5. The ability of the government to take and implement tough decisions dealing with economic reform. No new regime has scored here, but Poland is taking the lead in attempting to do so.

6. The extent of polarization between social classes, regions and ethnic groups. In most countries highly antagonistic groups are beginning to develop political consciousness and to mobilize for political purposes. The degree to which these cleavages will be destabilizing is unclear.

The future of democracy in Eastern Europe depends also on the nature of the governmental institutions that are developed; constitutional engineering becomes important here. It will also be shaped by the nature of the political parties and coalitions that emerge. Apart from Poland the situation seems to be one of the disintegration of communist parties and the fragmentation of their opposition. Groupings such as the Civic Forum in Czechoslovakia, the Democratic Forum and Opposition Round Table in Hungary, the New Forum in East Germany, and even Solidarity-as-a-political-movement were coalitions united by not much else than their opposition to the regime. The evolution of East European politics will depend in considerable measure on the answers to the following questions:

1. To what extent will opposition united fronts hold together and institutionalize?
2. To what extent will the opposition fragment into a large number of extremely small political groups lacking popular roots?
3. To what extent will reformers in the ex-communist parties be able to give these organizations a new lease on political life?
4. To what extent will a more familiar West European pattern of politics emerge, with parties representing liberalism, Christian Democracy, social democracy, reform communism, conservative nationalism and comparable tendencies?

The collapse of authoritarianism and the inauguration of democracy generate great enthusiasm. The workings of democracy generate indifference, frustration and disillusionment. The third wave is only 15 years old, but disappointment over the operation of democratic government has been widespread in Portugal, Argentina, Uruguay, Brazil, Peru, Turkey, Pakistan and the Philippines. This phenomenon appeared first in Spain, where it was labeled *el desencanto* (disillusionment), and that term is now used to describe the widespread feelings of alienation in Latin America. There and in the Philippines fledgling democracies have had to cope with bloated bureaucracies, debt crises, labor unrest, escalating inflation, great social inequalities, restless military establishments and, in some cases, major insurgencies. As of February 1990 all had survived, but several just barely.

In 1989 Eastern Europe also went through an explosion of popular participation and enthusiasm. The problems new East European democracies face will, in some respects, be less serious than those that have confronted new democracies in Latin America and elsewhere. Economic levels are higher, social inequalities less, military coups unlikely, insurgencies absent. *El desencanto*, nonetheless, will not be avoided. It is already manifesting itself. Behind the marches, rallies, caucuses and debates of the past year appear to be deep levels of political disillusionment and alienation and a strong desire by many to withdraw from politics. In several of the few elections that have been held so far the turnout has been small. Decades ago Central European theorists came up with the idea of "inner emigration" as a rational response to totalitarianism. It would be ironic if East European publics also found it a rational response to democracy.

■ The Breakup of the East European International Order

The decline in Soviet power and the dissolution of the Soviet contiguous empire have triggered major changes at the international level in Central and Eastern Europe. The freeze on East European international relations has melted. Initiative and control are no longer concentrated in Moscow. The sources of initiative have multiplied; the sources of control have vanished. The Soviet system is coming apart; the German nation is coming together. Soviet military power is receding; German economic power is advancing. The security threats of the future in East Europe will not come from the global rivalry of the two superpowers located on the European periphery. They will stem from the national and international politics of Central and Eastern Europe. The decline of the Soviet Union and the distance of the United States mean that the superpowers individually or jointly are likely to play marginal roles in promoting East European security. In the past, the Soviet-dominated international order insured domestic stability in Warsaw Pact nations, at times by the use of force. In the future, domestic politics within East European nations will shape international order or disorder in Eastern Europe. The lines of causation will run up rather than down. The democratization of power at the national level reinforces the diffusion of power at the international level. Already superpower arms control negotiators have to struggle to keep up with public pressures for the reduction or removal of military forces.

The breakup of the Soviet empire at the end of the Cold War bears certain resemblances to the breakup of the Hapsburg, Romanov and Hohenzollern empires at the end of World War I and the system now emerging in Eastern Europe could have some similarities to that of the 1920s and 1930s. There were two principal sources of instability in interwar Eastern Europe. The first, in the years immediately after World War I, involved diplomatic and military conflicts over territorial issues. Apart from the Burgenland dispute (Austria and Hungary) and the Fiume issue (Italy and Yugoslavia), these mostly concerned the borders of Poland. In the course of a few years the Poles fought the Lithuanians over Vilna, the Czechs over Teschen, the Russians over the Ukraine, and the Germans over Upper Silesia. Eventually, these disputes were resolved by a combination of negotiation, mediation and arms. The second principal source of international instability in the interwar period was, of course, German expansion in the 1930s. This led first to the incorporation and dismemberment of Austria and Czechoslovakia and then to World War II.

During the interwar years the states concerned with Eastern Europe attempted to cope with its instability potential through various patterns of alliances and guarantees. Three sets of association seemed to be particularly strong and/or recurring. First, the clubbing pattern involved the joining together of smaller East European states to protect themselves collectively against coercion or aggression by larger states. The Little Entente involving Czechoslovakia, Yugoslavia and Romania was the most notable effort along these lines, but the Balkan Pact encompassing Turkey, Greece, Romania and Yugoslavia was a somewhat comparable endeavor. Second, there was the condominium pattern in which the two local great powers, Germany and the Soviet Union, joined together to promote their own ends. The principal examples of this were the Rapallo and von Ribbentrop-Molotov treaties. Third, there was the sandwiching pattern, involving efforts to contain Germany by collaboration between countries to its east and west. The principal examples were the alliances between France and Poland and between France and the Little Entente. In the late

1930s Great Britain joined in this pattern with its guarantees to Czechoslovakia and Poland.

The security dilemma, however, was not absent from Eastern Europe. Clubs, condominiums and sandwiches might increase the security of the states that formed them, but other states inevitably saw their own security decreased. Hungary viewed the Little Entente as a threat. German-Soviet collaboration led to the elimination of Poland and the Baltic states. Germans necessarily saw the sandwiches as posing the threat of a two-front war, although the incredible disjunction between French diplomacy and French military strategy never made that a reality.

To what extent are the security threats and security arrangements of post-Cold War Eastern Europe likely to resemble those of interwar Eastern Europe? Fewer conflicting territorial claims exist now than in the 1920s, although certainly territorial conflicts could arise. The immediate issues concern less the rectification of boundaries than the treatment of minorities. The principal territorial issues now include the demands of the Baltic states for independence, the move of Slovenia toward secession from Yugoslavia, the potential demand for the return of Moldavia to Romania, and the Kosovo issue between Albania and Yugoslavia. The problem of the treatment of minorities exists in all these cases and also with respect to Hungarians in Romania and Turks in Bulgaria. The Macedonian question is also always there beneath the surface. The creation of new countries will exacerbate some minority problems, such as the position of Russians in the Baltic states. Overall, however, the brutal slaughter and expulsion of minorities during and immediately after World War II has, as Istvan Deak has pointed out, reduced the centrality of these issues as a source of instability in Eastern Europe.[5]

"The German question" has rapidly been redefined first as "the German challenge" and then as "the German threat." The immediate threat is not military but economic. East European countries want and need German money. They do not want to trade political domination by the Soviet Union for economic domination by a reunited Germany. To avoid this fate it is clearly in their interest to encourage the economic involve-

---

5. Istvan Deak, "Uncovering Eastern Europe's Dark History," *Orbis* 34 (Winter 1989), pp. 51–65.

ment in Eastern Europe of Japan, other EC countries (Italy, France and Britain) and the United States. The dangers of German dominance would also be reduced by the European Community assuming a central institutional role in promoting the economic development of Eastern Europe. Over time this could lead to deepening the association of East European countries with the Community.

The extent to which a unified Germany could pose a military threat to East European countries depends on its armaments and its alignments. A reunited Germany could be:

1. nonaligned and armed;
2. nonaligned and disarmed;
3. in NATO and armed;
4. in NATO and disarmed.

A nonaligned and armed Germany would be viewed as a threat by almost everyone else in Europe. A nonaligned and disarmed Germany would reassure the Soviet Union and East Europeans but would leave Western Europe exposed to a revival of Soviet militarism and would remove the stabilizing effect of the German-American connection. A Germany armed and in NATO would put German troops on the Polish border and be a threat to the Soviet Union and East Europeans. A Germany in NATO and substantially disarmed, on the other hand, would provide security assurances for almost everyone. Such an arrangement might involve:

1. the complete demilitarization of the East German part of a reunited Germany;
2. a drastic (50-percent or more) reduction in the size of the Bundeswehr;
3. a modest (50–75,000) U.S. troop presence in West Germany; and
4. membership of the reunited Germany in NATO.

A security arrangement of this sort would move NATO boundaries but not NATO forces from the Elbe to the Oder-Neisse. German security against renewal of Soviet aggressiveness would be provided by the NATO guarantee of the new eastern border, U.S. troops in West Germany and the small German military force. East European, meaning primarily Polish, security against German aggression would be provided by the East German demilitarized zone, the institutional constraints on Germany of NATO membership, the inhibiting effect on German action of U.S. troops in Germany and the security guarantees of the Warsaw Pact countries. An arrangement of this nature would also reduce, although not eliminate, the possibility of either a German-Soviet condominium threatening to the security of East European nations or a West European-East European sandwich threatening to Germany.

Security in Eastern Europe is likely to be enhanced by the continued existence of NATO and the Warsaw Pact providing mutual security guarantees among their members. The pacts, however, are likely to be supplemented by crosscutting economic and perhaps military associations. The Greeks and the Bulgarians are already cooperating against their traditional enemy, the Turks. The improved relations between his country and Greece, the Bulgarian foreign minister said, will be "a stabilizing factor in the Balkan Peninsula," but Ankara presumably has a somewhat different view.[6] The major West European countries undoubtedly will expand economic and cultural contacts and diplomatic cooperation with their traditional East European partners: France with Romania and Poland, Germany with Hungary and Czechoslovakia, Italy with Albania.

■ Conclusion: Democratization and Security

The democratization of power at the national level reinforces the diffusion of power at the international level. International security will depend, in large part, on the domestic stability achieved by the East European states. The principal danger democracy poses to security stems from the opportunity it gives political leaders and groups to appeal to ethnic loyalties and concerns. In democracies the passion of the populace can negate the statesmanship of their leaders. The actions of the new Bulgarian leadership in restoring the civil and religious rights to the Turkish minority produced mass protests and crowds chanting "Turks to Turkey!" and "Bulgaria for the Bulgarians!" Vaclav Havel's suggestion that Czechoslovakia should apologize for the expulsion of the Germans after World War II stimulated a nationalist reaction and promises that no apology would be made. Leaders of new political groups in Romania are demanding the retrocession of Molda-

---

6. See *The New York Times*, February 8, 1990, p. A9; *Time*, January 29, 1990, pp. 50–54.

via, and the leader of Europe's largest democracy, confronting an election later this year, has carefully refrained from stating that Germany's eastern border is fixed forever. The winding down of the Cold War has led a substantial plurality of Americans to view Japan rather than the Soviet Union as the principal threat to American security. The winding down of the Soviet empire is leading East European publics also to refocus on traditional enemies. The emergence of democracy in Eastern Europe may, in this respect, multiply the threats to East European security emanating from Eastern Europe.

Democratization can also make a more positive contribution to East European security. Democratic countries fight as many wars as nondemocratic countries and start wars as often as nondemocratic countries. Democracies, however, do not fight democracies. That, at least, is the historical record since the emergence of modern democratic states in the early 19th century. No generalization about politics is without exception, but the exceptions to this particular generalization are either technical (Finland formally at war with the Western Allies in World War II) or trivial (the "cod war" between Britain and Iceland). Democratic nations constitute a zone of peace. What has been true in the past is not necessarily true in the future, and Eastern Europe could be the exception to Kantian truth. The lesson of history, however, is that the surest way to security in Eastern Europe is the complete democratization of Eastern Europe.

5

The Role of the CSCE and the Council of Europe in Facilitating a Stable Transition Toward New Political Structures in Europe

EVA NOWOTNY

There are moments in history when everything changes, when established structures disappear and make room for something new. In European history, for instance, 1648 was such a turning point, as were 1814, 1914 and 1945; now we are witnessing another. What makes the present situation unique and without precedent in European history is the fact that all the previous major changes occurred after violent clashes and upheavals which brought down the old and brought forth the new. Today we are experiencing a different situation: structures are crumbling from within and the transformation is starting not as the result of an explosion, but rather an implosion, a collapse of the system from within. Like all the previous turning points, this situation offers great chances for progress toward greater security and more cooperation in a comprehensive European framework, but it is also not without risks of destabilization and fragmentation.

In her collection of essays *Practicing History*, Barbara Tuchman states that there are two ways of applying past experience: "One is to enable us to avoid past mistakes and to manage better in similar circumstances next time. The other is to enable us to anticipate a future course of events." In view of the very special circumstances with which we are dealing now, it seems to me that neither of these approaches is completely applicable. While it may be relatively easy to anticipate a future course of events according to one's own experience and expectations, the real task today will be to combine a set of very different expectations with a future-oriented pattern which can serve as a basis for political decisions today. It will not be easy to extract from our shared European historical experience many cogent conclusions from today's situation, but we can certainly analyze the instruments at our disposal with a special regard to "managing better." In doing so, one has to bear in mind the demands of the internal situation of the countries concerned, as well as the implications of each measure or set of measures for the continent as a whole.

I perceive two seemingly countervailing tendencies in Europe today. First, the thin and fragile bond of Soviet power and communist ideology which so precariously united the countries of Eastern Europe during the last decades has snapped. It did so suddenly and with a thoroughness that must have surprised even those analysts and politicians who have anticipated or predicted this possibility for many years. With the breaking of that bond, it has become apparent how little integrative spirit this enforced unity has created; apart from trade and military assistance, integration through the Warsaw Pact or the Council of Mutual Economic Assistance (CMEA) has never progressed beyond the essential minimum.

With new and sudden freedom and the return to democratic and pluralistic forms of government after years of one-party dominance, it is normal that the countries of Eastern Europe are trying to reconnect themselves to their own history; it is normal that they are trying to return to their "roots" in order to establish an identity, a sense of belonging and common purpose. All throughout Eastern Europe we are witnessing a return to the ideas, sentiments and even the symbols of a precommunist era.

Although this is a normal and foreseeable development, it also harbors a certain danger. Conflicts may flare up which have been dormant in the embrace of "proletarian internationalism," both inside the countries as well as in their relationships with each other; in some instances they have already done so. Were these conflicts to be used for domestic political purposes, for instance to generate national emotion in order to divert attention from domestic difficulties, this would not only have a very serious and harmful effect on security in the region; it would also promote an outdated concept of nationalism that is no longer suitable or equipped for dealing with the problems of today.

Second, in Western Europe the exact opposite trend is under way—the trend toward "Europeanization," toward new and ever further-reaching forms of integration and the slow but inevitable erosion of the sovereignty of the national state and all related concepts. Certainly there are populist/nationalist reactions opposing this trend in Western Europe as well, but they take a different form. The progress of European integration, the freedom of movement of citizens and the transfer of many national prerogatives to an anonymous cosmopolitan bureaucracy in Brussels have given rise to a revival of regional sentiments and regional consciousness in an effort to make up for the gradual decline of identification in the framework of the nation-state.

For Western Europe, the road into the future will be marked by continuous, if slow and difficult, progress toward increased integration, greater unity and larger structures. All the switches have been set in this direction. This tendency corresponds to the demands of the European economy and to developments in communications and information. It is best suited to deal with the great transnational problems of our time, such as the protection of the environment and the proper management of natural resources.

On this basis, what can be anticipated in the coming years? The optimal scenario would be a slow and gradual but purposeful development toward comprehensive European structures, toward the expansion of all-European institutions of cooperation that would be comprised of every European nation. In the interests of all concerned, West and East European countries alike, it would be most important to assure a gradual inclusion of the East European countries in the solid and multilayered network of West European cooperation and in the institutions that provide its structures and its legal backbone. Not only do they offer all the tools and instruments for the settlement of disputes and conflicts of interest; they also offer a great deal of accumulated know-how and experience which can be useful in the transition process.

There are a number of prerequisites for such a development. The Conference on Security and Cooperation in Europe (CSCE), as the Magna Carta of European stability, will have to adapt to the changed circumstances, but it will also have to continue and grow. The process of arms control, nuclear and conventional disarmament and the increasing orientation toward purely defensive strategies must be pursued with determination. This will require a strong and consolidated European

Community (EC) and European Free Trade Association (EFTA) to support the transformation in Eastern Europe. While pursuing this larger network of European cooperation, all forms of regional or subregional cooperation should be encouraged and developed. Alpe-Adria, or the "Quadrangular talks," recently started among Austria, Italy, Hungary and Yugoslavia could serve as a useful example in this respect.

What now are the instruments with which to approach this task? The most comprehensive framework for security, stability and cooperation in Europe today is certainly the CSCE process, which, as proof of its vitality and strength, has in its 15th year lost none of its importance or its attractiveness. The reason for this lies in the convincing, persuasive force of its underlying philosophy, namely that:

- peace and security can be achieved only through a network of long-term cooperation covering all areas of coexistence between states, and that only this kind of security can also support change and transformation;
- the practical effects of such cooperation must benefit every individual citizen; and
- cooperation and the tireless search for common solutions must take the place of confrontation and the search for unilateral advantages.

Through these basic concepts, the CSCE process guaranteed territorial stability and the inviolability of frontiers, while at the same time making the frontiers more human and more bearable. It assured a territorial status quo and removed old insecurities and fears. It became a driving force as well as a central forum for disarmament negotiations, verification and confidence-building. It addressed problems of the environment and of economic cooperation, and perhaps most important, the CSCE laid down accepted standards for the implementation of human rights and for the conduct of the signatory states vis-à-vis their own citizens.

Today it is an established fact that the CSCE norms and standards for human rights and political freedoms, which are accepted by all European governments, had a decisive role to play in the democratization processes in Eastern Europe. Certainly, each East European country is unique, and each experienced its own brand of revolution according to its national situation and experience as well as to the actors and forces involved. Each country has a right to the uniqueness of this experience and to be proud of its national achievement. Nonetheless, it is justified to assume that without the process of *perestroika* in the USSR and the subsequent change in the Soviet approach to European politics in general and its own security requirements in particular, as well as the achievements of the CSCE in the field of human rights and personal freedoms, the events of 1989 might easily have taken a different course.

A brief survey of some of the conclusions of the Vienna follow-up meeting of the CSCE exemplifies the wide variety of issues which have become part of the CSCE's mandate. A glance at the Final Document of the Vienna meeting reveals a new quality of the CSCE agreements which finds its clearest expression in the agreements on human rights and humanitarian questions. As a result of the changed political situation, many taboos of the past were swept away. The former often contradictory interpretations of human rights in the East and the West and the uneasy compromise that characterized CSCE decisions of previous meetings gave way to a joint position, in which the primary concern of the Western countries, the protection of the individual citizen against any infringement upon his or her rights by the state, found full reflection. Substantive agreements on human contacts, free travel, freedom of information and the working conditions of journalists point in the direction of greater openness and the free and uninhibited flow of information between East and West. Decisions relating to religious freedom, the protection of national minorities and the legal rights of the individual are necessary cornerstones for the development of pluralism and societies which are based on law and constitutional rights.

One of the most important results of the Vienna meeting, however, lies in the agreement on the supervision of human rights in and through every member of the CSCE, and in the creation of mechanisms for this purpose. With the general agreement on this extremely significant provision, the argument that concern for the implementation of human rights in any given state would constitute an unwarranted interference into its internal affairs has finally been discarded.

In the area of military security, the Vienna meeting's decision on negotiations on conventional disarmament constitutes a major step forward on a key issue of European security. Based on a realistic mandate that clearly reflects respect for the security concerns of East and West, these negotiations have developed and progressed in a satisfactory manner, with their conclusion expected for the fall of 1990. They are accompanied by negotiations on confidence-building measures, aimed at more openness and greater calculability of military activities and military potentials.

The hope of many participants that the meeting in Vienna would achieve equal progress in Basket II on economic cooperation and thus reflect the real importance of economic factors in East-West relations did not come true. Many of the decisions taken are stated in general terms and lack concrete recommendations. Nevertheless, they reflect the intention of the East European countries to move from centrally planned and controlled economies to free market economies, at the same time improving the framework conditions for expanded economic cooperation with the West. The texts on direct contacts between businessmen and entrepreneurs, on the uninhibited flow of information about the economic situation, joint ventures, direct investment and compensation show a clear assessment of the economic needs of Eastern Europe by the negotiators, as well as a new openness on the part of the governments concerned for new and higher forms of economic cooperation.

It is not without significance that in its Vienna meeting, the CSCE gave considerable attention to environmental questions. The growing importance of environmental concerns in Western Europe, with their inevitable impact on political decision-making, was met with a responsive attitude from the East European governments, where obviously the preoccupation with a rapidly deteriorating ecological situation is gaining influence. The Vienna document concentrates on cooperation in the fight against air pollution, in the prevention of as well as the mutual assistance in environmental accidents or catastrophes, and on the further elaboration of international law on environmental questions. The political power of these concerns was clearly shown by events in Bulgaria, where the 1989 CSCE environmental forum functioned as a starting point for the political transformation process.

The events in Eastern Europe in 1989 have drastically changed the political background of the CSCE. Originally conceived as an instrument to develop and further cooperation between the two opposing camps of East and West in Europe, the CSCE now can, as these differences fade, pursue the goal of a truly comprehensive, undivided Europe.

Occasionally it is argued that the CSCE is a by-product of the Cold War and thus a dated concept; that it has been negotiated by and through governments that have lost the respect and confidence of their people and will continue to carry a certain stigma in their regard; and that it would be wise to abandon it and create something better equipped to deal with the changing conditions on the continent. Certainly the CSCE will have to change and adapt to new conditions, a new set of priorities and a different framework of opportunities, but its new functions might be as important as its old ones.

In the years to come, the CSCE's importance as a stabilizing element in the transformation of Eastern Europe will continue to grow by offering to maintain a stable European environment in which these processes can develop and come to fruition. The CSCE is still the only successful comprehensive European endeavor in which all aspects of the peaceful relations of states, both to each other and to their citizens, are dealt with. It has brought to the continent a completely new understanding of security, it has developed an all-European consensus in the very sensitive areas of human rights and personal freedoms and it has opened the doors to an unprecedented climate of confidence and cooperation. Now more than ever, the transition of the East European partners to democratic government and the reform of the internal structures of these states requires not only stable conditions but also a great deal of assistance, know-how and expertise; thus it seems realistic to assume that the importance of the CSCE process will grow even larger.

It is reasonable to expect that security issues within the CSCE will continue to be of great relevance. In spite of its present difficulties, the USSR is still the most powerful of all the European nations. For the foreseeable future, it will be necessary to balance this power through continued U.S. involvement on the continent. Issues that touch upon the general questions of European security should, and most probably will, be dealt with in a forum in which the United States as well as the USSR participate as partners, but which nevertheless has a strong European direction and outlook. Only negotiations in such a forum can do justice to the issues at hand. This will concern mainly concrete and operational questions, such as the further development of conventional disarmament, the further elaboration of verification and confidence-building measures and the development of instruments for the settlement and prevention of conflicts, to mention only a few.

First and foremost, however, the present situation demands the establishment of a comprehensive European security system. Both military alliances are undergoing a change in their weight, cohesiveness and political influence; this is especially true for the Warsaw Pact. The impending reunification of the two German states can only be accommodated in a European order that comprises a strengthened European Community and a stronger institutionalized security system involving all European states.

In the field of economic cooperation, the need for the East European countries to duplicate as closely as possible all the institutions of economic cooperation in the West has become apparent. Were it possible to integrate these countries rapidly into this cooperative network, then Basket II of the CSCE might indeed become irrelevant. This, however, is not going to be the case. The transformation of the East European economies will require many things, and one of these is certainly time; therefore their accession to European integration will be a gradual one.

Bilateral negotiations between the East European countries and the EC have already started. In addition, EFTA has agreed to assist these countries to participate in the European free trade system to the extent possible, once the necessary prerequisites have been achieved. Both organizations are aware of their responsibility in this regard. One must not ignore, however, the fact that they are also going through a difficult transition phase of their own. The European Community's top priority is the completion of the internal market within a given time frame, which has been rendered more difficult by the political debate between "deepeners" and "wideners." Meanwhile, EFTA has embarked on negotiations with the European Community on the participation of its members in the internal market, thereby creating a "European Economic Space"—a time-consuming and strenuous negotiation process which demands a lot of attention and a concentration of forces.

In this transition phase the CSCE offers two advantages: it can be a forum both for the articulation and definition of the problems that have to be overcome and for making the joint decisions necessary to assist in this transitory period.

Relatively close cooperation between the CSCE and the Economic Commission for Europe (ECE) was already developed in the past; the CSCE established the agreed guidelines, while the ECE dealt with their practical implementation. This cooperation should be encouraged and developed, for practical purposes as well as because it offers a useful example of cooperation between two basically different institutions.

The economic forum of the CSCE, which began meeting in Bonn in March 1990, has clearly endorsed the major objectives of the transformation of the East European states to a free market economic system and, at the same time, has proved its awareness of the many political problems this transition will entail.

The scope of the CSCE's future activities in the field of economic cooperation ranges from technical questions—such as setting standards for statistics, facilitating agreements on the protection of investment, capital transfer or joint ventures and the development of industrial research—to questions of a more fundamental nature—such as the European energy situation and its prospects, questions of transit traffic, transportation and the necessary infrastructure, the future development of the Council of Mutual Economic Assistance and environmental protection.

It would, however, be shortsighted as well as superficial for the CSCE to focus only on security and economic questions, as important as they are. The transformation that has now started affects the whole societal fabric of the states, and there are many more areas in which assistance and acquired experience can be brought to bear.

One of the inevitable consequences of economic restructuring in Eastern Europe and the Soviet Union will be large-scale unemployment and related social hardships. All questions of social security will therefore gain a new dimension. The transition to multiparty systems will imply the development of new techniques of forming coalitions, reaching compromise and assuring its acceptance, thereby shaping consensus. The decline of the overriding influence of the communist parties entails the need to rebuild civic institutions, to rewrite and change the constitutions, to adopt a code of law and to adjust the educational system to a changed set of national priorities and learning requirements.

In the area of human rights in their broadest definition, Basket III of the CSCE will without a doubt remain a focal point, although—and this has already started—a growing number of tasks can be assigned to the Council of Europe. There is a good reason for this development. The CSCE defines itself as a forum of political negotiation and its various documents have the character of declarations of political intent, in which a certain standard is agreed upon and a frame of reference established. An institutionalization of the CSCE and the buildup of its institutional structures has now become inevitable, and a discussion of this question is already well under way. However, this will require time to be accomplished. The Council of Europe, however, is a supranational organ operating with legally binding agreements which have instruments for supervision and control.

The Council of Europe is not only the guardian of human rights and personal freedoms (the jurisdiction of the European Court in Strasbourg in these matters supercedes the jurisdiction on the national level); it has also created a large and important system of cooperation among its members in the fields of culture, education, harmonization of legal standards and documents, communication and information, social questions and the relatively new area of environmental protection. This system is constantly growing in a quiet, unobtrusive and unspectacular way.

In addition, membership in the Council of Europe offers a powerful symbolic value which should not be underestimated. In a way, membership certifies democratic status and grants the seal of approval to its members as European democratic states. Beyond its symbolic value, this seal of approval also has some practical importance: states that qualify for membership in the Council of Europe will also qualify for inclusion and participation in the other organizations of European integration.

It is an encouraging development that the Council of Europe has clearly stated its willingness to assume the new responsibilities that arise from the changes in the East European countries, and it is expected that Poland, Hungary and Czechoslovakia will in a relatively short time become full members of this organization. At its recent ministerial meeting in Lisbon, in which all East European countries except Romania participated, the Council of Europe approved the so-called "Demosthenes" program. This program was specifically set up to give practical advice and support to the East European countries in the process of democratization, to transmit the relevant standards for the Council of Europe and to help them prepare for full membership in this organization.

While the importance of the Council of Europe will grow with the inclusion of new members in its system of cooperation, one nonetheless has to be aware that there are limits to its future potential because of the continuing transfer of tasks to the European Community. This has become most apparent, for instance, in the field of scientific and research, where EC programs such as EUREKA and ESPRIT have pushed similar initiatives of the Council of Europe into the background. However, the Council's central role in the field of human rights, European parliamentarianism and codification and standardization of European law will remain unchallenged.

In conclusion, it is not expected that such a deep and difficult transition as that which has now begun in the East European countries can occur without internal and external frictions. In order to assure the continued stability and security of the European continent, which are also necessary prerequisites for the democratization process, it is most important to expand the existing network of multilateral cooperation through the gradual inclusion of the East European countries. In this process, a larger role for the CSCE, adapted to suit these new conditions, and for the Council of Europe offers a promising starting point for such a program of action.

6

Conclusion
PETER VOLTEN

In 1989 events in Eastern Europe developed a dynamic beyond anyone's imagination and, ultimately, beyond anyone's control. Beginning as a cautiously probing movement motivated by a general yet pressing yearning for democracy, social forces turned the events into a chain reaction. The election of a Solidarity prime minister in Poland, East Germans voting with their "feet" and the subsequent fall of the Berlin Wall, the "velvet revolution" in Czechoslovakia and the violent overthrow of the Ceausescu dictatorship in Romania marked the highlights of the genuine East European Revolution of 1989. It created the basis for democratic developments in the Eastern part of Europe and, as a consequence, the precondition for a virtually new European security structure. In the wake of the amazingly rapid and unanticipated change, a number of opportunities have emerged, as well as a number of unprecedented challenges.

What has to be overthrown is much clearer than the answer to the question of what will have to replace the obsolete and outmoded structures. Or, to borrow a phrase from our introduction, "transition from what?" is quite clear, whereas "transition to what?" will for some time remain an open-ended issue. It is important for analysis of the events first to recognize the distinct domestic and international features of the democratization process and second to comprehend their interrelationship and its impact on the emerging political order. The foregoing chapters are an attempt to do just that. They provide some answers to the many questions that suddenly confront us. They also lead the way to further inquiries of specific phenomena.

■ Domestic Survey

Regarding the internal dimension, the processes set in motion were, to quote Ralf Dahrendorf, "in the first instance processes of dismantling and destruction." Existing structures dominated by the center collapsed in the absence of a new institutional infrastructure. The ideal of the communist parties to impose a directed society increasingly had become the opposite: an *un*directed society.

Old social bonds completely shattered without new ones taking their place. In terms of values and global orientations the prevailing mood was indifference and, even within the ruling parties, ultimately fatal disbelief. Obviously the collapse of the center did not in itself guarantee the peaceful, structured and successful implementation of the economic and political goals of democratization. The withering away of the *ancien regime* did not lead automatically to democratic solutions. Today, many options are still open, including undemocratic, autocratic ones. The revolutions of 1989 did of course open the door for a number of great opportunities for the peaceful settlement of disputes on the basis of legitimate written and unwritten rules of policy. But the initial postrevolutionary period has also revealed various disruptive tendencies: indifferent, sometimes even negative attitudes toward politics in general and toward political parties (and not only communist parties) in particular; intolerance toward differing interests and opinions; ethnic violence and discrimination against minorities; and the emergence of new autocratic tendencies. This is hardly surprising since the lack of democratic traditions and 40 years of suppression of democratic values cannot be overcome overnight.

The time factor is crucial. First of all, the new political centers themselves will need time to overcome present weaknesses caused by the lack of tested institutional frameworks, in particular at the regional and local levels, and by the impact of the obsolete remnants of the old regimes. Faced with both widespread popular impatience and the reemergence of traditional ethnic, regional or religious rivalries, some governments may be posed with the challenge of maintaining law and order.

Furthermore, the establishment of a stable and legitimized social contract is hampered by conflicting time scales in the process of change. The time lag between political, economic and social transformations inevitably burdens the democratiza-

64

tion process and shakes the foundation of the new institutions. The admission and registration of new parties, new electoral laws and even a commission for constitutional change can be put in place within months, but the transition from the ill-functioning system of central planning to a market economy is not, in Dahrendorf's words, an "immediate positive-sum game." On the contrary, conditions will get worse before they get any better. It will probably take at least one government term of, say, four years before people will reap the first benefits of the inevitable austerity policies. Considerably longer periods of time will be necessary to prepare the ground for the most comprehensive transformation: the emergence of civil society. Here we will have to measure progress not in years, but in generations. With these time frames in mind, wisdom and patience on the part of both rulers and ruled are in high demand, indeed.

The notion of civil society, however complex, is crucial for the long-term peaceful and stable development of democracy in Eastern Europe. New rules, procedures and institutions alone are not sufficient; they should do justice to all participants in the polity. Moreover, the presence and functioning of independent groups and social movements and the acceptance and tolerance of differing interests are needed. In short, justice and pluralism should be part of the "constructive chaos of civil society."

The concept of civil society appears to raise more questions than it answers, in theory as well as in practice. Civil society— what is it? Can it be precisely defined? Can it be "created"? Is it evolving rather than being deliberately "built up"? Can governments help to "create" it? At a very fundamental level, civil society can of course be defined as one part of the twofold core of democracy. It represents the "corrective mechanism," whereas the rule of law as an institutionalized system of checks and balances including a strong and independent judiciary could be regarded as the "stabilizing mechanism." These mechanisms constitute a set of political-cultural habits developed into a complex and steady intellectual and organizational infrastructure for the "rules of the game."

Even if we examined cases where democracy actually works, it would be difficult to outline precisely the integral parts or even globally applicable features of civil society. A glance at the process of democratization in historical perspective can highlight general phenomena, as well as temper existing euphoria about the course of democracy in Eastern Europe. The successful transition to democracy is a rare occurrence and takes a very long time to consolidate. France is a prime example. In terms of the cultural prerequisites for a promising transition process, an egalitarian element in politics as well as a tradition of tolerance toward different interests and opinions are beneficial.

Regarding the prospects for democracy in the countries of the former Soviet bloc, three issues deserve particular attention. The first is connected with the absence of a middle class, which traditionally forms the social base for Western-type democracies. It is ironic that the intelligentsia, the driving force of the revolution, has subsequently realized that one of the foremost prerequisites for civil society is to "create" a bourgeoisie. But then again: can a bourgeoisie be "created"? The experience of the first period of the transformation process in East Central Europe, especially in Hungary and Poland, shows that bringing about a bourgeoisie is not as complicated as shaping a civil society. For example, the spectacular privatization of the state sector in Poland produced a class of entrepreneurs who might be called the new "owners of the old *nomenklatura*." Various combinations of the previous administrative and/or economic power and new capital facilities and market positions have generated the embryonic outline of a new bourgeoisie. Given the experience of some East Asian countries where the state played a large role in creating a new kind of entrepreneurship, it is reasonable to expect that this kind of political capitalism could form a pattern for building up bourgeois middle classes in the Eastern part of Europe.

The second area of concern results from a latent contradiction in Eastern societies that has begun to resurface. More than 40 years of "proletarian internationalism" had enforced the unnatural suppression of national and religious feelings, which understandably created a backlog demand for their free expression and exercise. As a consequence, already during their revolutions the countries of Eastern Europe witnessed a remarkable reemergence of traditional cultures. Subsequent postrevolutionary developments strengthened this tendency; the creation of numerous political parties purely on the basis of national affiliation is one of its most distinct manifestations. These waves of national revitalization clearly indicate that future political and social developments will be strongly affected by differences in cultural, psychological and political history. This already implies potential sources of splits and divisions, both within states, as was the case in the Czech-Slovak disputes about renaming the republic, and between states—witness the Hungarian-Romanian case. Resurgent interstate conflicts can have direct implications for international relations. Even a new cultural division between Central and Eastern—and possibly even southeastern—Europe cannot be excluded. This would have distinct repercussions on the democratization issue, perhaps leading to a relatively rapid rapprochement of the former parts of the Habsburg Empire (i.e., Czechoslovakia, Hungary, Poland and Slovenia) with Western standards, and the potential for an authoritarian relapse in other parts of Eastern Europe. Considering the range of predispositions it would be naive as well as counterproductive to expect a concept of democratization that could be applicable to all the countries of the region. Rather, different—and perhaps even conflicting—concepts of civil society and divergent roads toward democracy will develop.

The third set of problems refers to the character of political leadership. A strong orientation toward personalities rather than institutions is apparent. The charismatic appeal of Walesa or Havel dwarfs the requirement of qualifications in fields like the economy and foreign policy. Their personalities rather than their "professional" assets seem to be the key. Again we are witnessing an understandable yet possibly alarming legacy of the socialist regimes. For more than 40 years politics—in the real sense of the word—simply did not exist. Within the ruling parties and even moreso within the former opposition, political professionalism could not be generated or developed. Political talents could not be systematically taught the business of politics. As a result of the nonexistence of the art of politics, a generation of political appointees rather than politicians was installed. Only now are the beginnings of normal political life taking shape, and it seems clear that forming a new generation of accountable, well versed politicians on all governmental and party levels will be a time-consuming process. Meanwhile, the lack of professional politicians contributes to the kind of problems connected with reservations about assuming genuine political leadership. Although the existing fear of strong central political leadership is understandable in view of 40 years of experience with overcentralization, now is the time for real leaders, embodying liberation and hope, in Eastern Europe. There is a yearning for leaders with a political vision that is inextricably bound up in the notion of civil society.

■ *The International Survey*

In both East and West, domestic politics now have primacy over foreign policy. In Eastern Europe in particular foreign policy will for the time being be greatly dependent on domestic developments on the road toward democracy. So now, more than ever before, is the future order of Europe. Moreover, as Europe's previously bipolar relationships grow increasingly multipolar, the emergence of a new correlation is evident: the process of democratization on the national level reinforces the diffusion of power at the international level. In other words, greater influence of domestic politics on the all-European (and even global) political order means that the problems described above may be a source of international instability. In the long term, a flourishing democratization process in the Eastern part of Europe will reduce the dangers of instability. In the short term, however, incalculable developments lie ahead in a Europe where *Realpolitik* and even vulgar power politics between uncertain as well as mature democracies may again become preeminent. The way to new power relationships in as well as between East and West is likely to be a conflict-prone process.

As for the European security system, the revolutions of 1989 and the change in the USSR since 1985 have led to a dramatic change in the balance of forces. Although it may be premature to outline precisely what the new political architecture of Europe will look like, some of its most obvious features are already becoming clear. Previously, the link between the United States and its West European allies rested on a foundation of close military cooperation. The Soviet military threat was the cement that held the Western alliance together. Economic ties played a secondary role. As the military relationship becomes less urgent, however, the economic and political dimensions will become a more visible and pronounced part of transatlantic relations. Washington, if it wishes, will remain an influential, though not decisive, player on the European scene. Meanwhile, in the Eastern part of Europe, the relationship between the Soviet Union and its former satellites has been destroyed. Soviet power has decreased rapidly and dramatically.

At the core of the question of Europe's future lies the issue that currently dominates the political agenda: the reunification of Germany. The outcome of the reunification process as well as the conditions that will be attached it will do much to determine future political relations among the European (and North American) states.

At present, two possible scenarios for German reunification seem to prevail, one leading to the construction of a united Europe, the other toward a fragmented Europe. In the first, the construction scenario, the process of integrating a reunited Germany into a more united Europe, one based on current institutions such as the European Economic Community (EEC), NATO, the Western European Union (WEU) and the Council of Europe, would proceed smoothly. Germany would then assume the role of an economic superpower, but it would not pose a credible military threat to the security of either individual European states or to the stability of Europe as a whole. As a result, the West would feel secure and confident in dealing with instabilities and unforeseen developments in Eastern Europe and the Soviet Union. Moreover, Western Europe would conduct a fairly well integrated foreign policy and would be capable of supporting the political and economic developments in the East. At the same time, countries in Central Europe could establish an alliance along the lines suggested by Samuel P. Huntington: a Central European Democratic Organization (CEDO). Such an alliance could be built on four areas of common interest: 1) military security; 2) national and minority questions; 3) strengthening new democratic institutions; and 4) facilitating all-European political and economic cooperation.

In the second scenario, the fragmentation scenario, Germans would set their own terms for both the internal union of the FRG and the GDR and a reunited Germany's external relations with its neighbors and allies. In this scenario, existing European institutions would be likely to become distorted as the Germans used their economic power, unrestrained by either a powerful American presence in Europe or by a credible Soviet military threat, to position a reunited Germany at the center of the process of all-European integration. Germany would set both the pace and conditions for this process. All of this would take place in a Western Europe which would have become fragmented, because both the American-led NATO and the collective leadership of the EEC would have disintegrated. This, in turn, would have serious consequences for the prospects for smoothly integrating the East and Central European countries into the new all-European political structures. An alliance between a "neutral" Germany and the Central European Democratic Organization mentioned above would be a move toward the fragmentation of Europe.

These two scenarios are rather extreme examples of what could happen to Europe in the future. Certainly the construction scenario would be the preferable solution. But who decides? In the history of international relations decisions are usually portrayed as being dealt with on a government-to-government basis. However, as the experiences of 1989 have shown, it is impossible to ignore the attitudes and actions of the populations of all the countries involved in defining the new Europe. People are no longer content to have their futures decided over their heads and they will be heard from both on the street and at the ballot box. In the GDR, for example, the rapidity of change and the March 1990 elections have shown the enormous impatience of the people and their too long restrained yearning for material improvement. "The primacy of material interest," as George Schöpflin reminds us in his contribution, should not be underestimated. Finally, governments that forget the forceful popular leap toward a democratic community of states in Europe do so not only at their own risk, but also at the risk of missing an extraordinary chance in international relations.

The assumed prerogative of governments to decide upon national and international issues has also been gradually eroded by multilateral institutions and organizations. Western Europe has steadily moved toward closer cooperation in a variety of fields and the individual countries have appeared to be ready, albeit reluctantly, to give up some of their sovereign rights in favor of international rule. This trend should not only be actively pursued among the Western states, but be extended to the emerging democracies in the Eastern part of Europe. The creation of a democratic international community, however, faces serious obstacles in both East and West. In contrast to the admittedly slow but voluntary devolution of national power in the West, the events of 1989 are likely to reinforce the desire to exercise sovereignty, freedom of action and independence in the East. The liberation from 40 years of an imposed, zero-sum style of integration may—for some time at least—lead to the resurgence of native traditions and national pride. However understandable such a trend may be, it is not conducive to the creation of a solid community of societies in Europe as a whole.

Material or other conflicting interests in the West may not work in favor of democratic internationalism either. Yet the experience of voluntary multilateral cooperation and international institution-building is well founded. After many years in which devotion and indifference as well as belief and disbelief come together in a process of trial and error, cooperation and integration in Western Europe seems irreversible. Obviously, institutions such as the EC, the Council of Europe, the European Free Trade Association (EFTA) and the Organization for Economic Cooperation and Development (OECD) will play a part in strengthening the all-European democratization and integration processes. They could help shorten the passage through the "valley of tears," ease domestic polarization and pave the way for European citizenship. All of these steps would be crucial contributions.

Clearly, then, multinational institutions, individual governments and social forces will all continue to play a part in reshaping the European political order. Each of their contributions to a democratic, cooperative arrangement will be partial and imperfect, sometimes leading to progress and at other times to setbacks. But there is no alternative; there is no international body that exists or can be invented that can carry out the mission of comprehensive change toward democratization and institution-building in Europe. Existing powers would resist such a superinstitution and the idea of a new organization would at best remain a disappointing concept or at worst revive the false expectations of the League of Nations and the United Nations in the aftermath of the two world wars.

Of the existing frameworks for democratization and institution-building in Europe, the Conference on Security and Cooperation in Europe (CSCE) has been and will probably continue to be the most comprehensive one. All participants in this forum can act as equals. The CSCE process has significantly contributed to change and transformation by focusing on human rights issues, the peaceful resolution of security and border questions and military transparency in East and West. For many observers, strengthening the present CSCE framework would therefore be the most obvious way to safeguard the balance of change and stability.

One should recognize the CSCE's shortcomings as well. The CSCE framework was developed in the context of bipolar, antagonistic security structures. Some of its characteristics retain the weakness of those times of confrontation. The CSCE functions at the level of the lowest denominator, its decisions are not legally binding and bilateral agreements still prevail over multilateral ones. The CSCE provides no legal framework; it is only a process that can lead to legal arrangements. The current CSCE process would have to undergo significant changes and include new forms and forums to become an institutionalized framework for the business of European integration.

Indeed, we are talking about the necessity of a businesslike approach. On the part of the West, nothing would be more counterproductive than a pedantic or monopolistic approach, nothing more shortsighted than the impertinence of superiority. Western support in both general/theoretical as well as more practical terms should be directed to (at least) the following aspects and levels:

- building up a middle class as the most important and the most reliable social basis for democracy;
- reinforcing approaches that strengthen national identity and self-confidence but resist nationalistic temptations and that build bridges between conflicting national or religious groups; and
- educating a democratic leadership on all respective levels of government and administration, with particular attention to spreading this process to the level of local authorities.

In Central and Eastern Europe a strong desire to learn from the democratic experiences of the West does exist, but not at any price. Interest and support, rather than obstructive interference, are what the East asks of the West. Institutional frameworks at all levels—multilateral, government-to-government and societal—are needed to bring pluralism, justice and civil society to the East and cooperative security to both East and West.

Both of these tasks are fundamentally important, albeit for the time being they are not equally balanced in their interdependence. Without pluralism, democracy and civil society in the East, no stable all-European cooperative security structure will be possible. Or, to put it in a very concrete form, without a process first toward control and subsequently toward reconciliation in the relations between Romanians and Hungarians, progress within the CSCE process will remain endangered. Patience is needed on both sides given the necessary period of social transformation which is a precondition for national reconciliation, as the example of Franco-German relations shows. But the first steps must be taken, and this process needs support at all levels, including the international one. Thus the task of the CSCE and other supranational institutions and processes must also undergo a visible change, leading them to include internal developments more broadly in their agenda. Not only the future of individual countries but the future of Europe and European cooperation depend on the fate of pluralism, justice and civil society in the countries of Eastern and Central Europe.

ABOUT THE AUTHORS

Ralf Dahrendorf is Warden of St. Anthony's College at Oxford University and former Director of the London School of Economics. Elected to the West German Bundestag in 1969, he served as a Minister of State in the West German Foreign Ministry. In 1970 he served in Brussels as the European Commissioner for Foreign Trade and External Relations. He has written numerous books on politics and social democracy. His most recent book was *The Modern Social Conflict* (1988).

Eva Nowotny is Foreign Policy Advisor to the Austrian Federal Chancellor. She has held several positions in the Austrian foreign service, including First Secretary at the Austrian Embassy in Cairo. From 1978 to 1983 she served as Counsellor for Political Affairs and Security Council Affairs at the Austrian Mission to the United Nations.

Samuel Huntington is Eaton Professor of the Science of Government and Director of the John M. Olin Institute for Strategic Studies at the Center for International Affairs at Harvard University. He served as Coordinator of Security Planning for the National Security Council from 1977–78 and has held positions on many national commissions on strategic issues and problems of international development. He has written extensively on military politics, strategy and civil-military relations as well as American and comparative politics and political development in less developed countries.

George Schöpflin is Lecturer in the political institutions of East European Politics at the London School of Economics, University of London. He has published extensively on the problems of political development in Eastern Europe, specifically in Hungary.

Biographical Sketches
Warsaw Meeting

Dr. Jozsef Bayer is Senior Researcher at the Institute for Social Sciences in Budapest, where his main fields of interest are political theory and sociology. He also heads the department for research on social consciousness, and leads a national research project on this topic. He has lectured for four years at the Institute of European Studies in Vienna on East European political systems, and has written extensively on the subjects of democracy, pluralism and ideology.

Professor Gyorgy Bence is Associate Professor in the Department of Humanities at Elte University in Hungary.

Sir Ralf Dahrendorf is Warden of St. Anthony's College at Oxford and former Director of the London School of Economics. Elected to the Bundestag in 1969, he served as a minister of state in the West German foreign ministry and in 1970 served in Brussels as a European Commissioner for foreign trade and external relations. He has written several books on politics and social democracy, the latest of which is entitled *The Modern Social Conflict* (1988).

Professor Dr. Vyacheslav Dashichev is Head of the International Relations Department at the Institute of World Economics of the World Socialist System in the USSR.

Dr. Magarditsch Hatschikjan is Research Associate at the Institute for East-West Security Studies in New York. Formerly of the Research Institute of the Konrad Adenauer Foundation, he has held the title of Guest Lecturer in East European history at the University of Dusseldorf since 1987. His fields of specialization include comparative communist political systems, Soviet and East European foreign policy and nationalism and national minority conflicts in Eastern Europe. He has written several articles on the effect of Gorbachev's policies in Eastern Europe, including "Prag und die Furcht vor der Umgestaltung," which is forthcoming in "Wehrausbildung."

Ms. Rita Hauser is Senior Partner at Stroock & Stroock & Lavan in the United States. She has served as US Chair for the International Center for Peace in the Middle East since 1984, and has been a member of the State Department Advisory Panel on International Law since 1986. In addition, from 1984 to 1988 she chaired an advisory group for the International

Parliamentary Group for Human Rights in the Soviet Union, and served as US Public Delegate to the Vienna Follow-up Meeting of the Conference on Security and Cooperation in Europe from 1986 to 1988.

Dr. Ivan Havel is a member of the Executive Committee of Civic Forum in Czechoslovakia.

Professor Germaine Hoston is Professor of Political Science at The Johns Hopkins University. A specialist in comparative politics with an emphasis on Japan, China and the Soviet Union, she has written extensively on Marxism in Japan and China, and has participated in numerous academic panels on these subjects. She is currently writing her second book, entitled *Marxism and the National Question in China and Japan: Nation, State and Revolution in Asia.*

Professor Samuel Huntington is Eaton Professor of the Science of Government and Director of the John M. Olin Institute for Strategic Studies at the Center for International Affairs at Harvard University. In addition to his distinguished academic career, he served as Coordinator of Security Planning for the National Security Council from 1977–78, and has held positions on many national commissions on strategic issues and problems of international development. He has written extensively in the following areas: military politics, strategy, and civil-military relations, American and comparative politics, and political development in less developed countries.

Mr. Andriej Ivanov is at the Institute of History of the Bulgarian Communist Party.

Professor Georgi Karasimeonov is the Head of the Department of Political Systems at the University of Sofia.

Dr. William Korey is Director of International Policy Research for B'nai B'rith International, and is currently preparing a study on American policy and the Helsinki process on a grant from the Ford Foundation. He is the author of several books and numerous articles on human rights and the Helsinki process, including *Human Rights and the Helsinki Accord* (1983).

Professor Wojtek Lamentowicz is Founder and President of the Independent Center for International Affairs. He is also Associate Professor of Law at the University of Warsaw, and a member of the Solidarity Citizens' Committee, in which capacity he advises Prime Minister Mazowiecki on foreign policy issues. He is the author of *Legitimacy of Power in Postwar Poland* (1988) and has co-authored many books on the philosophy of law, political sociology and international relations.

The Honorable William Luers is currently the President of the Metropolitan Museum of Art. In his distinguished career in the foreign service, he served as Ambassador to Czechoslovakia from 1983 to 1986 and Ambassador to Venezuela from 1978 to 1982. He has also served in the State Department as Deputy Executive Secretary and Deputy Assistant Secretary of Inter-American Affairs, Deputy Assistant Secretary for European Affairs, and Deputy Directory of the Office of Soviet Affairs. He has written extensively for various newspapers and magazines on the Soviet Union and Eastern Europe, East-West relations and Latin America.

Ms. Edwina Moreton is at the Foreign Department of *The Economist* in London.

Professor Robert Mroziewicz is Associate Professor at the East European Research Group in Poland and Deputy Editor in Chief for the political quarterly *Krytyka*. In addition, he is a member of Solidarity. His research interests include contemporary history, international relations, and US diplomacy in the nineteenth and twentieth centuries. He is the author and co-author of several books and articles on these subjects.

Dr. Eva Nowotny is Foreign Policy Advisor to the Austrian Federal Chancellor. She has held several positions in the Austrian foreign service, including First Secretary at the Austrian Embassy in Cairo. In addition, from 1978 to 1983 she served as Counsellor for Political Affairs and Security Council Affairs in the Austrian Mission to the United Nations.

Dr. Krzysztof Ostrowski is the Director of the International Bureau of Social Democracy of the Republic of Poland in Warsaw.

Professor Maciej Perczynski is Director of the Polish Institute of International Affairs.

Dr. Adam Daniel Rotfeld is Senior Researcher at the Stockholm International Peace Research Institute, and a member of the Public Advisory Committee to the Polish Foreign Minister since 1988. He was a member of the Polish delegation to the second stage of CSCE talks in Geneva from 1973 to 1975, as well as the follow-up meetings in Belgrade and Madrid, and was Deputy Head of the delegation in Vienna from 1986 to 1988. In addition to participating in many international conferences and seminars on European security, he is the author of numerous monographs and articles on European security. His most recent publication, *From Confidence to Disarmament* (1986), was awarded by the Polish Academy of Sciences in 1988 as the best book on peace and security published in Poland.

Dr. Aleksei Salmin is Head of the Department for Comparative Research in Political Processes at the Institute of International Labor Studies in the USSR. Originally an Oriental specialist, he now does comparative research on Eastern and Western political culture. His main areas of interest have been problems of social mobility, the political behavior of French industrial workers, and ethnic problems in the Soviet Union. His latest work is entitled "The Political Culture of Social Democracy" (Moscow, 1987).

Professor George Schoepflin is Lecturer in East European Politics at the London School of Economics.

Dr. Vasile Secares is Vice President of the Commission on Foreign Policy for the Council on National Salvation in Romania. He is former Associate Professor in the Department of International Relations in the Stefan Gheorghiu Academy in Bucharest.

Dr. Ryszard Stemplowski is Research Fellow at the Institute of History in the Polish Academy of Sciences and East European Research Group in Poland. His areas of interest are Latin American and Eastern European history and international relations. In addition to his membership in several professional associations in the US and Europe, he is the author of several books and articles on these subjects, and is also the editor of the journal *Estudios Latinoamericanos*.

Mr. Max van der Stoel is a Member of the Council of State of the Netherlands. In addition to holding several terms in the Upper and Lower Houses of the Dutch Parliament, his distinguished career in government includes two terms as Minister for Foreign Affairs, from 1973 to 1977 and from 1981 to 1982. He has twice been a member of the North Atlantic Assembly and was a member of a select group to study the future of NATO in 1972–73. From 1983 to 1986 he was Permanent Representative of the Netherlands to the UN, and last year served as Netherlands Representative to the CSCE conference on the Human Dimension in Paris.

Dr. Peter Volten is Director of Research at the Institute for East-West Security Studies. Previously he was Director of Studies and Strategic Planning of the Defense Staff of the Dutch

Defense Ministry in the Hague and Professor of the History of War at Utrecht University. He has written extensively on security and defense matters with a special interest in the Soviet Union and East-West relations.

Professor Klaus Ziemer is Associate Professor at the Institute for Political Science at the University of Heidelberg; since 1986 he has served as guest professor at the Universities of Essen, Munich, and Mannheim. He is the author of several articles on political and social reform in Poland, including "Poland After the Referendum—Blind Alley or Chances for Further Reforms?" (*Das Parliament*, 1988) and "On the Way to Systemic Change in Poland" (*Osteuropa*, 1989). His latest work, "The Change of Political Legitimation in Poland," is soon to appear in *Sudosteuropa*.